Funny Funny Funny

Also by Denys Parsons in Pan

Funny Ha Ha and Funny Peculiar
Funny Ho Ho and Funny Fantastic
Funny Convulsing and Funny Confusing
Funny Amusing and Funny Amazing

Denys Parsons

FUNNY FUNNY FUNNY

A Pan Original
Pan Books London and Sydney

First published 1976 by Pan Books Ltd,
Cavaye Place, London SW10 9PG

ISBN 0 330 24714 X
Printed and bound in Great Britain by
Hunt Barnard Printing Ltd, Aylesbury, Bucks

Introduction

For new readers, unacquainted with the hilarious exploits of Gobfrey Shrdlu, I must explain that Shrdlu is the mischief-maker who lurks at the elbow of journalists and printers, causing misprints, double meanings and general mix-ups.

I also hold Shrdlu responsible for another type of curious happening, exemplified by the headlines: 'MAN BITES HORSE', 'UNBORN BABY SWALLOWS A BULLET', and 'PIGEON NESTS ON GLADYS AT HYMN TIME'.

Once again I acknowledge my debt to *Weekend*, *Punch* and *New Yorker*, in which some of the items first appeared, and also to my readers, especially three loyal shrdlologists, Edward North, Mary Pearce and Patrick Moore.

As in the previous four books in this series, the misprint items (Funny Ha Ha) are generally arranged on left-hand pages, and the oddities (Funny Peculiar) on right-hand pages. Gobfrey Shrdlu suggests that the best way to enjoy them is for one member of the family to read the items aloud to the others.

Funny Ha Ha

Funny Peculiar

PETER OOSTERHUIS shot a Manchester United manager, who joined West Ham as a scout, will not be on the payroll. He'll just collect expenses.

Evening Standard

Paul Kelly of Lime Avenue, East Grinstead was fined £15 at East Grinstead Magistrates Court on Monday for using a colour television without a silencer.

East Grinstead Observer

MAN RECOVERING AFTER FATAL CRASH

Limerick Weekly Echo

Lunch on this trip will be provided free on account of the fact that the cost has already been added to the original price of the ticket.

Canary Island brochure

ENGLISH GREEN THREE SEATER lounge suit as new $700. Phone S-pore 39844.

Advert in *Straits Times*

The AA was also called to the aid of a helicopter in Hampshire yesterday. 'The pilot was a member and we always like to help a member in a jam, even if he is nit in a car.'

Daily Express

The fact that West Wickham fire station is situated in a road which is blocked at both ends was mentioned by the Secretary of Hayes Village Association on Thursday last week.

Kentish Times

All my life I have suffered from very hairy ears. Two years ago a friend told me that this was because I was a Liberal. This so impressed me that I joined the Socialist Party, and now I have very hairy backs to my hands too.

Letter in the *Daily Mail*

'People,' he commented, 'don't hang from their bedroom windows late at night, screaming for some considerable time, because they cannot have relations with their wives.' He thought it had been proved that this was what Mr W— had done.

News of the World

A SKITTISH Northern lady who would prefer to be nameless arrived home the other day to find her husband working on his car. He was lying underneath it with his legs sticking out and as she passed she said 'Hello, darling,' and gave him what you might call an intimate squeeze.

She then proceeded in high spirits into the house, where, to her horror and astonishment, she met her husband in the hall. Meanwhile the man next door had sustained a wound to his forehead that required three stitches. He found it hard to explain to HIS wife why he had banged his head so hard on the underside of his neighbour's car.

Evening Standard

First check the tyres for cuts and blemishes. Now get down on your knees, move them backwards and forwards, and if there is any appreciable shake, that indicates worn bearings or swivel pins.

Motor Mart

In a luxury car, naturally you'd expect a radio, carpets, sophisticated air ventilation and heating, cigarette lighter, a clock, and bird-proof door locks.

Herald, New Zealand

The intruder was cornered by a polite dog.

Wimbledon News

As a State School-educated MP with personal experience down the mines, the Queen should get an interesting slant on the day's proceedings.

Evening Standard

Maxim de Winter himself is a difficult character to portray since he has to persuade us that he is truly haunted by the sceptre of his old wife.

Slough Observer

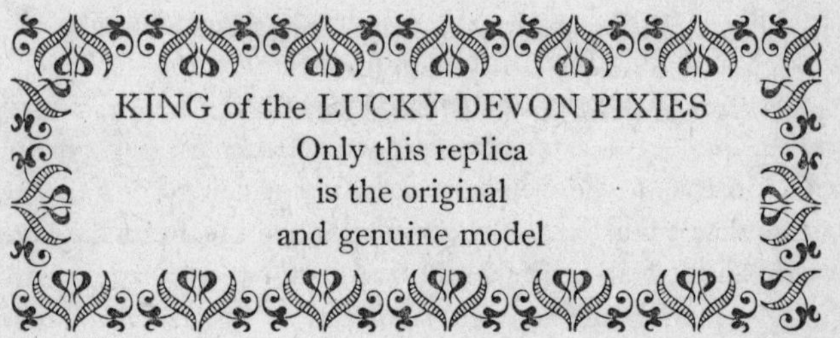

Advert card

The magistrate, Mr Harley, said he thought it proper that at times a man should beat his wife, and the Bible supported that statement; but beating must be done as a service of love, not in temper. Accused should have used a reasonably sized stick. It was a pity he had lost his temper and used an iron bar.

Daily Telegraph

The fifty girl operatives who went on strike in a Belfast bakery on Monday afternoon because they were refused permission to sing at their work by the management resumed their duties yesterday. The management has modified its ban on singing and now permits the girls to hum.

quoted in *New Statesman*'s 'This England'

From Brig Sir MARK HENNIKER

SIR—Mrs Mary Stewart-Wallace's letter (April 12), preferring 'referendums' and 'mediums' to 'referenda' and 'media', reminds me of the lightning reply made by a famous sapper, when a subaltern, to a pompous scientist.

The question was: 'Have you two officers completed your experiments with the pendula?'

The reply: 'Yes, sir. We are now sitting on our ba doing our sa.'

MARK HENNIKER

Letter to *Daily Telegraph*

Mr Leonard said PC Groves told the detectives, 'I was repairing her needlework-box and accidentally hit her on the head. Somehow it developed and I put my arms round her neck and strangled her. Have you ever had one of those days when nothing goes right?'

The Times

A police Alsatian dog which tickled an armed man was at Bow Street Court today, given £1 reward to be converted into juicy marrow bones.

Derby Evening Telegraph

A MAN said by Bri-Biggs, the last of Bri-bers still at large, is be-tish police to be Ronald tain's great train rob-hind bars in Brazil.

Sunday Herald, New Zealand

IN MEMORIAM
Large bathroom heater, vanity 26.1.72. Lovingly remembered by Vera and Jane and Jack Wilson

Gosford Star

Weekend Weather Outlook: Becoming colder. Wind SW moderate. Rain in moist areas on Sunday.

Essex paper

Sir, – After seeing the Royal wedding on TV, I think 'God Save the Queen' should be retained as our National Anthem, together with our own 'God Defend New Zealand'. Both could be played simultaneously at State occasions.

Evening Post, Wellington, NZ

WANTED: man to wash dishes and two waitresses.

Notice in Sydney restaurant

NOTICE TO CAMPERS

Peace is wished. Therefor are not allowed musicplaying, Singing, using of radios, laud screams and yells, bambling of carroseries, and so on. Also have a thought for the sleaping people when it is 22 p.m., so dropp washing clothes or bits at that time, for the running water is noisy.

Please protect the bushes, don't cut off trees or branches. Don't build up wild walls of soncs or crabbs around your place. The stuff it is made of is blowen with the wind and disturbs everyone. Digging waterholes is not to do either. The one who does it has to planificate the spott before leaving.

We wish you a pleasurefull and peacefull subjourn. – If you are in need of a help or feel like to slay up a wish, please you are welcome to us.

Notice at German camp site, quoted by Paul Jennings in *Daily Telegraph*

A MOTORIST stopped an RAC breakdown van near Oxford yesterday and asked for a nut and bolt two-to-three inches long.

Patrolman Elliott obliged – and watched as the man fitted it to his artificial leg, walked up and down to test it, said 'That's just right' and drove off.

Daily Mail

GEOFF LEWIS, a 49-year-old Essex factory foreman, had a problem: his left foot was size 9 and his right, 7½. He put an ad in a local paper: 'Gentleman with odd-size feet wants to contact another with opposite requirements.' Schoolmaster Douglas Presland, aged 48, of Thorrington, Essex, came to the rescue. Mr Lewis declared happily: 'Now that I've been paired off we can agree on styles and swap the ones we don't need through the post.'

Daily Mail

The record player is the first item which the members hope to buy – to liven up the club – and they will set about looking for other unnecessary equipment.

The Mail, Hartlepool

Seaford did well against their uneaten opponents.

Sussex Express & Herald

TO LET FURNISHED: self-contained flatlet: £30 per calendar month; hot water, lighting, rats inclusive.

Advert in *Liverpool Echo*

She had come to his house to use the phone. He had only kissed her on a Disprin for a headache he had at the time.

Southern Star

The crew christened the bird Captain Cook and their skipper took him home and lodged him in a cake with the family pet budgie.

Sunday Sun, Newcastle

All staff must leave the building by the appointed fire exits, in an orderly manner (unless individually instructed otherwise).

Fire drill instruction

One of her first duties was to present Mrs Jackson, retiring president, with a gift, a silver ice bucket and tongues from the members of the institute.

Ormskirk Advertiser

Sir, Having just attended an excellent performance of Gilbert and Sullivan's *Patience* at Sadler's Wells I write to ask whether any of your readers think I could take action against the D'Oyly Carte Opera Company under the provisions of the Trade Descriptions Act.

During the performance of the song 'Twenty lovesick maidens we', at no time did twenty maidens appear; indeed the number was three short, thus an obvious misrepresentation of the facts.

Yours sincerely, Robin Ollington

Letter to *The Times*

VIOLINIST Franz Achfeld arrived at a Vienna concert hall with a bandaged head, and he was asked what had happened. He explained: 'I began tuning my violin at my new lodgings when the landlady stormed into my room and accused me of trying to move the bed, because, she said, she had heard the squeaking noise the bed made when shifted.

'I explained that I was merely tuning my violin, and she said that if that was what my playing sounded like, she would tear up the ticket she had bought for my concert. I swore at her, and she broke a chamberpot over my head.'

Tit-Bits

HAIFA, Israel: An Arab accused of sending a coded telegram to inform Egypt that Israel was mobilizing reserves was said to have been paid 12 umbrellas for his services.

Daily Mail

The breakfast cereal that goes 'Snap! Crackle! Pop!' when the milk is added would in fact be going 'Cric! Crac! Croc!' in France, 'Pif! Paf! Puf!' in Holland and 'Knisper! Knasper! Knusper!' in Germany.

Tit-Bits

> Pukerua Bay: House, fibrous plaster, 3 large bedrooms, septic tank not quite complete. Owner living in same.

Dominion, New Zealand

Ensign and Mrs William A. Clark have announced the girth of a son, Kenneth William, on Oct 6th at Neenah, Wisconsin.

Montclair (New Jersey) *Times*

He smiled and let his gaze fall to hers, so that her cheek began to glow. Ecstatically she waited until his mouth slowly neared her own. She knew only one thing:
rdoendtrgoveniardgoverdgovnrdgog.

Badische Presse

After the dinner Mr Khrushchev led Mrs Eisenhower by the arm down the Embassy steps, while President Eisenhower took Mrs Khrushchev's ars. The Soviet Prime Minister was smiling broadly and obviously enjoying himself.

Essex paper

After my marriage I taught a class of backward children in a county primary school. I feel I have the right kind of training and experience to understand your problems and represent you on the City Council.

From an election address

Sun-Suit Schoolgirl Is
Suspended By Head

North London paper

Signal from Destroyer to unknown Trawler:

WHAT IS THE SIGNIFICANCE OF THAT SIGNAL YOU ARE FLYING?

From Trawler:

REGRET I DO NOT KNOW. FLAGS SMELT OF FISH.

from *Make a Signal* by Captain Jack Broome

It is suspected that this police practice would not exist if the scales of the system were not presently loaded so much in favour of defendants and we have a classic case of the escalating vicious circle.

The Times

TWINS Christine and Carol Foster, from Chandler's Ford, Hampshire, on a hitch-hiking holiday in Italy, each broke a leg yesterday when a 66 lb Parmesan cheese fell from a lorry and struck them after rolling down a slope.

Guardian

The woman thought she was buying a cactus. But when she got the bill it was for an umbrella. So she complained to the store, David Morgan's in Cardiff. And they sent her this explanation:

Account customers please note. You have been served with your cactus by our Rainwear Staff. We have unfortunately been unable to teach our Computer the difference between an umbrella and a Cactus. Therefore, on your next monthly statement, your cactus will be described as an umbrella.

Daily Express

TRAINING IN ORAL CONTRACEPTION

London. July 17, 10 a.m. to 4 p.m. at the Royal Society of Medicine, 1 Wimpole Street, W1. Notify Mrs White, stating if lunch required.

Announcement in *British Medical Journal*

Five thugs last night pulled the British passenger ship *Capetown* clear of the sandbank on which she went aground at Flushing early yesterday.

Belfast Morning News

School lessons in the lavatory

By our Correspondent

Overcrowding is so bad in the village school at Cefn Mawr, near Wrexham, that a class takes its lessons in the lavatory. A Denbighshire education authority official said yesterday. 'The children will not have to endure conditions like this for long. A new £700 toilet block is to be built.'

Guardian

The MV *Siglion* is the longest ship ever built at Laird's. Her length overall is 820ft. The naming ceremony was carried out by Mrs Doris B—, wife of Mr Simon B—, and despite her giant size, she moved smoothly into the waiting waters of the Mersey.

Birkenhead News

The dog was seen swimming around unable to get out of the water at Brierly Hill. The police were old and they asked the fire brigade for help.

Wolverhampton Express and Star

Frog eater jumps clear

SELF-CONFESSED professional poacher Derek Podmore flapped into court yesterday in a frogman's suit with flippers, and with pheasant feathers behind his ears. He pleaded not guilty to a charge under the Cruelty to Animals Act 1911 – to wit, swallowing a live frog in the lounge of the Railway Hotel, at Market Drayton, Shropshire.

Journalist witnesses said Mr Podmore, who plans to beat the world record (five frogs in 65 seconds) swallowed an adult frog with a draught of black-and-tan.

A veterinary surgeon, Mr Elved Jones, said the frog would die from suffocation or possibly shock. Death would be slow and cruel. The magistrates took two minutes to acquit Mr Podmore of causing unnecessary suffering, but refused to allow him costs.

Daily Express

Surely it is common sense that Nature intended us to sleep in contact with the earth. Instead, we build artificial dwellings insulated from the earth, and then we wonder why we get all sorts of nervous ailments. Sleeping two storeys up, I nevertheless manage to keep my body at earth potential by attaching the wireless earth. Sometimes I wrap the bare wire round my waist, and sometimes I wrap it round my big toe.

This simple expedient does away at one sweep with thousands of years of artificial living, and anyone who tries it will notice that his dreams are much more vivid.

Letter in weekly paper

Powerful personality, clear voice and imposing stature made her the perfect Queen of the Fairies.

Aberdeen Evening Express

An official not telling of the attempt to deliver the parcel was pushed through the letterbox.

Dublin Evening Press

They were accompanied by the air attaché from the Royal Swedish Embassy of thumping music.

Evening Star, Ipswich

The village pond is being cleared out and the chairman said there was plenty of evidence that sewage had been getting into it. Abingdon RDC is to be asked to wee that this does not happen again.

North Bucks Herald

Ladies! We are looking for cafeteria assistants to work in our modern cafeteria in the Grive Road area. Successful applicants will be asked to work occasionally.

South Wales Argus

Such delights will not be seen on Bournemouth's sands this summer. The town council has refused to allow nude sunbathing on part of the beach. Councillor Mrs Gladys Bell summed up: 'I know we want to be regarded as a swinging town, but we touch bottom when we come to this.'

Weekend

'We have a family pet dog called Paddy,' she said. 'A cross between a collie and a surgeon's bills when we get them.'

Western Morning News

The bridegroom was accompanied by Mr John Taylor, and as they entered the church Miss Jones, who was at the organ, played bridal music, which at the bridegroom's request was interspersed with strains of 'Rescue the Perishing'.

Scillonian

● **Gerona. Here is a name and a symbol. A name set in the tentacles of Empire. Of aristocratic craddle. Old and fruitful savour, speaking about daring legions, unfinishing ways, acqueducts, warlike marching and toges. Gerona was promise and reality. Promise because upon it would fall the evangelic seed, the seed of the mustard, not because small less strong in the aborescence and the fruit.**

From a Gerona guidebook

THE SECURITIES and EXCHANGE COMMISSION, an American government supervisory agency for stock exchanges and brokers, yesterday filed suit to prevent a German business group from selling stock in a brothel to Americans. The SEC claims that the proprietors, Hans-Wolf Peiper and Monika Knipple, failed to justify their claims that investors could get a 100 per cent return within 10 months.

Guardian

A Canadian divorce court heard that for two years Drew Sunley and his wife, Rosemary, did not speak to each other in their Toronto flat.

They communicated by tying notes to the tail of their golden labrador, Bondy. The dog spent its evenings trotting from one bedroom to the next.

Tit-Bits

Under this law it would be illegal to display in a street or other public place any written, pictorial, or other material which was held to be decent.

Greenock Telegraph

Specially aimed at theatregoers visiting London from out of town, buses leave Piccadilly Circus every evening except Sundays.

From a theatre programme

Mr and Mrs John Beverlin are rejoicing over an eight-pound daughter, their sixth child since last Saturday.

Illinois paper

The large spectacles that he wore half-way down his hooked nose did not dispute the fact that the latter were red with weeping.

Daily Mail

Miss Georgina P. Mathie, principal psychologist, County of Stirling, quoted the case of a nine-year-old boy who ran amok with a hatchet in the large family of which he was a member, saying, 'There are far too many bairns here.' She showed how by psychological treatment he became completely adjusted and several years later was working a guillotine in a printer's establishment.

Ross-shire Journal

The man who would stoop so low as to write an anonymous letter, the least he could do would be to sign his name to it.

Letter in Irish paper

Jack Sales, medical student and member of London Hospital Rugby team, admitted at Penzance today that while touring the West Country with the team he took a barber's pole from outside a shop and took it to bed with him.

Evening Standard

'My husband cut himself so severely in forcing open the children's money-box that he had to spend the contents on lint and bandages.' *Evening News*

'We booked a girl with big, firm breasts,' said the producer of a tobacco commercial. 'The idea was for her to be filmed bra-less so that all the male viewers would be turned on by her nipples pushing through her thin, tight sweater.

'We took her 200 miles to a lonely beach with twenty technicians and equipment worth thousands of pounds. Then we discovered that her nipples didn't perform as they should. The girl started crying and said that she'd never, ah, stood out in that way. It was obviously going to cost too much to abandon shooting and book another girl, so we stuck a couple of rubber thimbles where her nipples should have been.

'The result: sensational. Now she complains that boyfriends who have seen her on the screen only take her out for one thing, or rather two things, and they are disappointed when they find the truth.'

Daily Mirror

Mr Stenson of Redditch applied to Redditch Urban Council for permission to erect a telephone pole in his garden. The Estates, Baths and Cemeteries Committee, before whom the application was set, decided to defer the matter while they explored the possibility of transferring Mr Hirst to a house which was adjacent to an existing telephone pole.

Birmingham Despatch

The competitors were in no way upset by the cold north-east wind blowing on the diving-board from the four corners of the earth.

Daily Mail

Ickes declared: 'It should be thoroughly understood that the Solid Fuels Administration is not trying to convert anthracite consumers to the use of bituminous coal. We are trying to convert anthracite consumers to the use of bituminous coal.

Springfield (Massachusetts) *Evening Union*

A reception was held at the home of the groom and the happy couple left afterwards for their honeymoon at Coleshill near Birmingham. The bride travelled in her birthday outfit.

Blaydon Courier

Dr T— had been heard frequently to refuse to put into his pocket that which he felt ought to go into the stomachs of his patients.

Berkhamstead Gazette

Many other brides in the collection are scheduled as ancient monuments.

Bath paper

Mrs Skeffinton regrets not being able to keep her appointment with Dr James owing to sickness today at 12 o'clock as arranged.

Note to Liverpool doctor

'I never meant to do her any harm,' Smithers told the judge, 'and I was the first to pull her out.'

The judge said: 'You must not go shoving Mrs Kitchener into the canal every time she takes her dog for a walk.'

'Oh no, sir,' said Smithers indignantly. 'I wouldn't see the dog drown.'

quoted in *New Statesman*'s 'This England'

So the congregation resolved upon a European trip for their beloved pastor, and on Saturday made him acquainted with the delightful fact. Accompanying the report of the Committee was a nicely filled purse, which was placed at the disposal of the pastor, who, after thanking them, made a turn down South Main Street as far as Planet, then up Planet to Benefit Street, where he was caught by some boys, who tied a tin pan to his tail. Away he went again, up Benefit Street, and down College, at the foot of which he was shot by a policeman.

Providence Daily Journal

Messrs E. and A. Heim, having investigated the tones of waterfalls, state that a mass of falling water gives the chord of C sharp, and also the non-accordant F. When C and D sound louder than the middle note, F is heard very fully, as a deep dull humming, far-resounding tone, with a strength proportionate to the mass of falling water. It easily penetrates to a distance at which the other notes are inaudible. The notes C, E, G, F belong to all rushing water, and in great falls are sometimes in different octaves. Small falls give the same notes one or two octaves higher. In the stronger falls, F is heard most easily; in the weak ones, C. At the first attempt, C is most readily detected.

Persons with musical cultivation, on attempting to sing near rapidly moving water, naturally use the key of C sharp, or of F sharp, if near a great fall.

Scribners, 1875

The dispensary, however, will be open in the afternoon from one-thirty to four on Monday to Friday for decapitated students with the nurse in charge.

Pomona College Student Life

Couple, expecting September, require house, flat, furnished, unfurnished, so babe may live in manner to which has been accustomed.

Courier Mail, Brisbane

★ CHEAP SPONGE ROLL ★

Take a teacupful of flour and mix it with a teacupful of caster sugar and a teaspoonful of baking powder; break two eggs into a cup, then slide into the mixture.

Bristol Times and Mirror

After removing the meat from your broiling pan allow it to soak in soapy water.

Seattle Post-Intelligencer

Some 13,500 other American citizens are now playing nursemaid to these South American rodents, envisioning wealth beyond the dreams of Ava Rice.

Pittsburgh Press

I once got a circular from a man who grew potatoes containing his photograph and, I think, an autobiography.

Musical Standard

A Danish court granted Leah Kjeld a divorce because her husband, a butcher, stripped her and chased her through the streets, slapping her bottom with a heavy sausage. She had burned his dinner.

Tit-Bits

Mrs Bell gives the signal

When Mrs Bell, 50, cleaner, porter and ticket collector at Small Heath, Birmingham, wants to go to the lavatory, this is the procedure laid down by the National Union of Railwaymen:

She phones the train recorder Mr Alexander Priest in the nearest signal box. He walks 200 yards to the station, walks back with her to his box, where there is a lavatory, waits, escorts her back to the station and then returns. The NUR says that the floorboards in the station lavatory are unsafe. And under railway regulations Mrs Bell may not walk unescorted along the line.

Daily Mail

At the instance of the veterinary service of the Dordogne all the wild rabbits are to be vaccinated against myxamotosis. If they do not report at the office of the Departmental Federation of Hunters the local authorities are requested to capture them at their warrens by using ferrets.

Eclaireur du Gâtinais

A woman who poured petrol over her sleeping husband and set fire to him was cleared of manslaughter and arson yesterday.

Daily Mirror

Practise thinning in winter time and head back in summer. A tree can be kept bearing practically regular crops. Of course it is impossible to keep any tree bearing practically regular crops, but of course it is impossible to keep any tree bearing a full crop regularly. Wonders can be done by this system of pruning.

Nurseryman's leaflet

Mrs Alice McCrory and son, Harvey, went to Drayton last Sunday to visit Mr and Mrs Carl Dunbar, who were slightly injured in an automobile accident last week. Mrs Dunbar before her accident was Miss Olivia McCrory.

Ohio paper

The will disposes of a million-dollar estate, the bunk going to relatives.

Washington Star

PARISIAN BEHEADED FOR KILLING WIFE BEFORE MISTRESS

St Louis Post-Dispatch

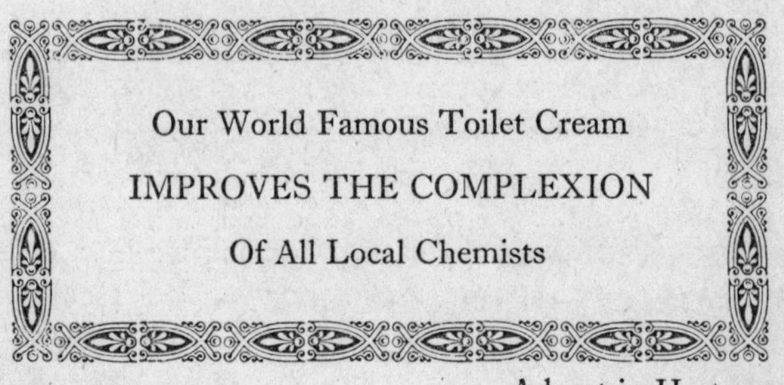

Advert in Herts paper

The mayor of Hennebont, yielding to the repeated demands of the local people that the WC at the entry to the extension of the trunk road should be removed, has decided that it should be demolished by 16 October. Interested parties will therefore have to make their own arrangements.

Ouest-France quoted in *La Réalité dépasse la fiction*

To put an end to certain malicious rumours whose motives are well understood, Mme Mabelle of Menneville wishes to inform the public that her bull has been examined by a vet, and that, if there is in the neighbourhood any creature suffering from a shameful disease, it is not her bull.

Echo de Mont-Moulin

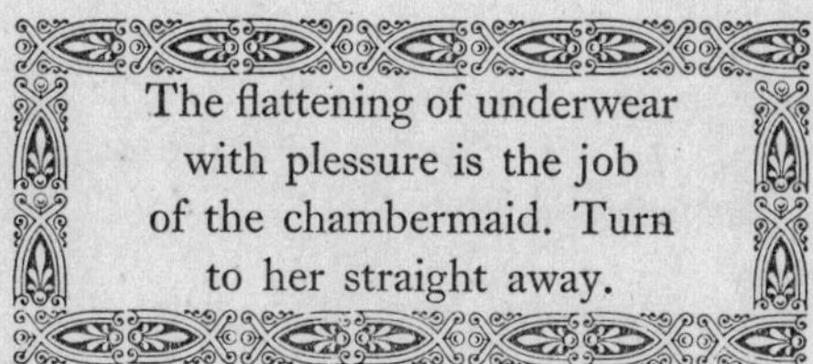

Hotel notice in Brno

Because she believed Christ was in her car, Mrs D— of Perivale pleaded not guilty to driving unaccompanied and with no 'L' plates at Hendon Court on Monday. 'The invisible man was driving my car,' she said, 'and I know that was Christ who guided me. He was sitting in the car with me and supervising my driving.' 'I am a Christian,' she said, 'and I know I have not done wrong.'

Finchley Times and Guardian

This is an interesting and absorbing position for a secretary with the right personal qualities which include complete discussion in dealing with confidential matters.

Sunderland Echo

The macaw of Honduras says a lecturer resembles many people in wearing fine clothes, making a great noise, and in being good for nothing else.

Evening News

DETACHED PRIVATE HOTEL

EXCELLENTLY SITUATED

near Torquay Sea Front
Practically on the level

Advert in Devonshire paper

Mrs Edgar Ramsden was rushed to Roanoke Hospital on Monday of this week for observation and treatment prior to becoming an expectant mother.

Virginia paper

On making enquiries at the Hospital this afternoon, we learn that the deceased is as well as can be expected.

Jersey Evening Post

All-round good working
man wanted to take the
place of a Ferguson
tractor and two small
horses.

Advert in Bucks paper

His Lordship said that the parties were married in 1946. The marriage had, in its later stages, been the subject of a remarkable history of litigation. It had made a powerful contribution to the legal history of this country and had added a great deal to our knowledge of the law of cruelty.

The Times

A 60-YEAR-OLD grandmother has been banned from attending any more soccer matches at her town ground. Mrs Alice V—, of Stourbridge, Worcs, has been accused of 'ungentlemanly conduct' by the committee of Southern League Club after an incident at the end of their home game with Weymouth. The club has been ordered to appear before an FA disciplinary commission to answer a charge of crowd misconduct.

During a scuffle Graham Williams, former West Bromwich Albion and Wales, now player-manager of Weymouth, was punched in the mouth and a linesman was struck with a rattle. Mrs V—, whose son has also been barred from the ground, claimed yesterday that the ban was unfair. She said she had shouted at Williams during the game when he charged the Stourbridge goalkeeper. 'He waved two fingers at me.'

Daily Telegraph

NOTICE

Will gentlemen taking pots of tea on to the college lawns please exercise more care.
Their hot bottoms are killing the grass.

University notice

COUNTLESS OTHER WORLDS

Dr Jones's argument for believing that there are countless other worlds where living beings are present, briefly, is this:

Ninety per cent of the shrimps served on the tables of the United States come from the coastal waters of Alabama, Florida, Georgia, Louisiana, Mississipi, and Texas.

Minneapolis Tribune

☞ We make a speciality of gorillas and chimpanzees. They are wonderfully intelligent and can be trained right up to the human standard in all except speech. One of our directors, Mr Taylor and his wife are both able to be tamed to live in captivity.

Irish paper

We welcome news of Old Boys, particularly those who have died.

Devon school magazine

WANTED – A steady young woman to wash, iron and milk two cows.

New Zealand paper

Keen educated young woman wants Agriculture or part Agriculture and Secretarial work in Blandford area. Three months' farm experience, good shorthorn typist.

Advert in West Country paper

As per an inscription found in Bologna, L. Clodius Hermippus is said to have reached an age of 115 years by breathing on young girls. The author takes the occasion and analyses thoroughly the phenomenon of the prolongation of life by blowing. Simultaneously he writes on general dietetics.

Zentralantiquariat der DDR

The shape of an egg is perfectly adapted to its function, a wonderful example of the application of aerodynamic principles to an object which moves slowly. Cubic eggs, for example, would make a hen's life impossible.

Familial Digest

What You Must Not Do

To walk around alone or in groups, in an inadequate form and adapting attitudes that denote a personal bad state, to offend the elemental civil conduct.

To make noises and scandals in the sight of the public and establishments.

Sit down or lie down in sight of the public, to obstruct the freedom of the people.

Utilizing ponds, fountains, for personal use.

To break or tear objects in the sight of the public or crowded places.

To utilize percussion instruments after midnight.

Festival handbill, Pamplona

My budgie, a guaranteed cockbird, according to the breeder, went down the neck of my dress, settled halfway down my anatomy and there laid an egg! A strange experience!

Letter in *Competitors Journal*

Mrs Joe Sexton and children, of Deadwood Gulch, were guests of the A. Dennys family on Sunday.

Mrs Dennys is almost confined to her bed with nervous exhaustion.

Idaho paper

The captain swam ashore from the vessel and subsequently saved the life of the stewardess; she was insured for fifteen thousand dollars and was full of railroad iron.

California paper

In addition to the fine work done by the Irish regiments he assured them that many a warm Irish heart beat under a Scottish kilt.

Irish paper

A roast chicken an American woman had bought as a gift to a friend in Brixton Prison was found stuffed with cannabis resin, South Western magistrates were told yesterday.

A second chicken was similarly stuffed but refused to say who it was intended for.

Daily Telegraph

Joe lifted his eyes quietly a moment to hers then sat down to his coffee. Without opening his mouth again, he finished this, hesitated, arose . . .

Story in American magazine

Wash beets very clean, then boil. When done, swim out into a pan of cold water and slip the skins off with the fingers.

Boston Globe

Man shows dog how to bite a policeman

ANDRÉ TILLON was a little disappointed with his dog. It wouldn't bite three policemen who were about to arrest him. So André set it an example by leaping forward and sinking his own teeth into one of the officers. The policeman finished up with a deep bite in the hand.

A puzzled André said when the policeman had calmed down: 'I always thought my dog was fierce, but he let me down this time.' André, a Paris restaurant owner, had been stopped by the officers at the weekend, apparently driving under the influence of drink. As they walked up to him, 38-year-old André brought his redsetter out of the car and ordered, 'Attack.'

But the dog didn't move – and that, a Paris court was told later, was when André's false teeth started snapping. André told the court that he was not his normal self because his 14-year-old daughter was ill. André was jailed for six months and lost his driving licence.

Daily Mirror

A death with honour decision was made by the North West Sussex Water Board at Horsham yesterday. A directive to the board's bailiffs allows them to shoot cormorants suspected of eating any of the £1,700 worth of trout which are to restock Crawley's Weir Wood reservoir at Forest Row. But 'to be fair' to the dead birds a post-mortem examination will be made to establish their guilt or innocence.

Guardian, quoted in *New Statesman*

When a youth went to a girl's home her mother gave the girl a pair of scissors to cut his shoulder-length hair. Instead of doing so properly the young people had sexual intercourse together.

South London Press

Tomorrow week the Canadian regimental doctors will be deposited for safe keeping in Bristol Cathedral.

Bristol paper

VIOLENCE - JUDGE HITS OUT

Nottingham Evening Post

In 1918 he was appointed business manager of the Great War at a salary of £15 a week.

West Country paper

Policeman Leo Grant was shot through the stomach and John Marcinoak, taxi driver, through the hip, while a trusty at the jail was shot in the excitement.

San Francisco Call-Bulletin

FUNERALS

 Parking for clients only 

Notice at Surrey undertakers

One unusual feature is a so-called bachelor's chamber with a private bathroom. The maids' bedrooms and bath are conveniently located and are reached by a private stairway.

Newhaven Journal-Courier

In last week's issue of the *Falmouth Packet* we published details of a Penryn resident's encounter with a porpoise climbing the steps at Penryn Quay. This was an incorrect report due to a bad telephone connection. What the man really saw coming up the steps was a coypu, an animal which is similar in appearance to a large rat or an otter. We regret any inconvenience which we may have caused by our erroneous report.

Falmouth Packet

At a neighbour's suggestion I tied old sacking around the base of my apple tree to trap insects. The first time I moved it I found hundreds of earwigs. Just as I was about to destroy them I remembered reading that earwigs are devoted mothers, risking anything to protect their young. I replaced the sacking without killing one. Needless to say there isn't an apple fit to eat.

Letter in the *People*

A Spanish snail named Pepe sped over a track just over a yard long in five minutes to set a new world record and win the second international snail derby, it was reported in Madrid today.

Pepe outdistanced 75 competing snails from seven other countries in the northern Spanish village of Murillo de Rio Leza. His feat was so surprising that the organizers of the international snail derby pardoned the lives of the other competitors, waiving their previous rule that snails left at the post would wind up in the pot in the all-night snail feast following the race.

from *The Times* by permission

Appropriate music was played on the organ by Mr G. E. satin with pearl trimming. Her train was that on earth do dwell' and 'Father now Thy grace extending.'

The bride was becomingly attired in white Good. The hymns sung were 'All people of silver lace, and she wore a tulle veil, which had been used at her mother's wedding.

Local paper

House and shop for sale; tenant under notice to expire end of March.

Welsh paper

The service was conducted by the Rev Peter S—. After the Benedictine, Mr and Mrs Taylor sang 'I'll walk beside you.'

Report of wedding

To bring wives over by telephone without permit, consult Mr R—, Marine Superintendent and Receiver of Wrecks.

Notice at Naval Base

Why rend your garments elsewhere when our up-to-date laundry can do the work more effectively?

New Zealand paper

He was asked if he contemplated any further act of matrimony. 'Certainly,' was his evasive reply.

New York World

CLOTHES BRUSH The genuine pigskin back opens with a zipper and inside are tweezers, scissors, nail-file, and a bomb.

Canadian paper

Does anyone have a spare pelvis and a couple of thighbones he doesn't want? If the rest of the legbones are attached, so much the better. I need them to teach mountaineers how to walk. The hip should roll with a circular movement, but this, to be demonstrated by a live person, must be exaggerated and the effect is indescribably sexy. An old skeleton is ideal for the purpose.

Letter in the *Sun*

At all events Breconshire seems the one place where maternity beds ought not to be at a premium in March. Elsewhere the situation is different. 'I'm sorry, sir,' a colleague was told by the almoner of one Midland maternity hospital in September, 'but if your wife needs a bed in March it should have been booked 10 months in advance.'

The Times

Mrs Johnstone said she never saw an axe in her husband's hand – 'I could just feel myself being hit,' she said. Detective Constable John French said that when he cautioned and charged Johnstone, he replied: 'I should have killed her and got it done with. Anyway did you hear how the Celtic got on?'

Glasgow Evening Citizen

Police Constable Roy Barkins, booked by a fellow policeman for parking, told Ipswich magistrates yesterday, 'I had to attend this court as a witness. I knew that 20 minutes is the parking limit except with special permission from a uniformed policeman. I was in uniform and there was no other policeman about so I gave myself permission.'

Daily Mail

In recent weeks the services have been conducted by the Rev Thomas owing to the continued illness of the Vicar, which we trust is reaching its last stage.

New Zealand diocesan magazine

January 20th, at Kenyon Road, Wavertree, to Mr and Mrs Oswald Unsworth, a son (bath well).

Liverpool Echo

Chauffeur-handyman, aged 40; wife Vienna cook, occasionally one child.

Advert in *Morning Post*

Striking testimony to the popularity of the Cataract Cliff Grounds is the fact that during the first five years an aggregate of 428,390 persons was bitten by a snake.

Tasmanian paper

Mrs A. P. Payne will not be at home today, owing to her absence from home.

Brisbane Courier

TICK BITE FEVER APPEARS TO BE DUE TO BITE OF CERTAIN TICKS

American Medical Association News

LADIES CORSET BOARDS

Some weeks fince, I fpent a few days in the flourifhing village of Waterford, a romantic little place, was delighted with the fituation – manners of the people very agreeable; treat ftrangers with great attention and politenefs. One evening, I accompanied a young gentleman who was very polite, to a room where many young ladies had gathered together, called a *tea party*; I was politely introduced to all in the room. After being feated a fhort time, I was not a little surprifed to fee fo many fine looking girls, the picture of health, all apparently troubled with the *Rickets*. I muft confefs my feelings were excited to pity, whilft meditating on the misfortune of human life; the young lady which appeared to have the rickets much the worft, fuddenly fainted, and was infenfible of any thing; fome cried throw water in her face; fome one thing and fome another, *all was confufion*! One lady which appeared to be more fenfible of the caufe of her fainting, drew from her bofom a *board about half a yard in length*, from *three to four inches wide* – The lady immediately revived on the board being removed. After the blufter was over, I was fatisfied that I had formed a wrong opinion, that they were troubled with *boards* inftead of the *rickets*. Fearing there might be more fainting, I excufed myfelf and left them to converfe upon the misfortune of being under the difagreeable neceffity of *drawing the board*.

Young ladies, are you fo fimple and ignorant as to flatter yourfelves that you can alter your frames and fhapes for the better. Has not your CREATOR formed you in his own likenefs, made you to perfection – an ornament to the world? – *And are you ftill diffatisfied*? – Woman is the nobleft work of God. Does your vain imagination whifper to you, that 'you can mould your frames fuperior to that which nature has done

continued on page 43

Miss Y—, the well-known singer, was nearly poisoned at one time. So she said at the meeting on Tuesday. When she said she had been nearly poisoned, the features of the members expressed regret.

Irish paper

Thanksgiving Day, Thursday, November 24th, will be observed with the Service of Morning Prayer at 9 o'clock. The choir will sing appropriate music. There will not be a sermon, Let us Thank God for Our Blessings.

Harrisburg, Pennsylvania, church notice

Just for a change of pace, serve diced cooked carrots and peas in a cheese sauce to which a little finely grated opinion has been added.

Waterbury American

Two tablespoonfuls of paraffin oil added to the footpath will relieve and refresh aching feet.

Dorset paper

Already the Governor has begun applying for sick leave, showing that internal difficulties are rampant.

Far Eastern paper

He's the same type as his son – forceful, aggressive, wanting to do things and get things done and above all, anxious to sin.

North Western Evening Mail

Although every possible care has been taken, I do not accept responsibility for inoccurancies.

Malta guidebook

for you?' – Oh blufh for fhame. Many of your fex, whilft in the midft of gaiety and health, have undertaken to accomplifh a work of this kind – Divine Providence has frowned upon them, and they now lie mouldering in the duft. Let this be a warning to you and profit by it.

If you wifh to be fenfible and wife, efteemed by your friends, and loved by your God, never undertake the arduous tafk which you can never accomplifh to form or mould a frame fuperior to that which your Maker has made in his own likenefs.

A STRANGER
Waterford (N.Y.) *Gazette*, 1816

I expect to meet my dog in the next world, but not the thousands that have been in the Battersea Dogs' Home of which I am not presently conscious.

Letter in *Sunday Times*

BANGKOK, Tuesday. – The hunt is on for a 30-year-old woman who last week in a fit of jealousy cut off her husband's penis with a razor blade, wrapped it in paper and caught a bus for Udorn Thani, 650 kilometres north-east of here.

According to police the incident took place while Mr S— B— lay sleeping in their home in Bangkok's Dusit district before dawn, after the wife discovered her husband was having an affair with a neighbour's wife. B—, who was rushed to hospital for emergency treatment, was reported to be in fair condition yesterday.

Police did not explain whether doctors will try to rejoin the penis when Mrs B— is arrested. The couple has three children.

Far East paper

The children in the junior school start at 8.50 a.m. and finish at 4 p.m. If this arrangement continues next year the eighty-year-olds who will remain in the first school will lose 3 hours 20 minutes a week of schooling.

Harrow paper

A strong link between the driving records of fathers and their sins has been discovered by two researchers.

New York Daily News

The zoo will be open this week unless wildcat strike resumes.

Philadelphia Inquirer

The slow movement was beautifully managed – the closing bars especially spell-binding – and the finale taken briskly but with great rhythmic control and with plenty of time for the subtitles which abound in the movement – a fresh and exciting reading.

Bristol paper

Will the individual who borrowed a ladder from the caretaker last month kindly return same immediately, otherwise further steps will be taken.

Notice in Leicester village hall

Replied Mrs Mavres' counsel, Mr Frank Cridlan: 'This is a A two-tailed new 2p piece woman from Cyprus where the women's liberation movement has not yet made many inroads.'

Daily Express

Mr C. E. Hall: We should have a public convenience irrespective of who is going to use it. It is a sign of civilization to have one in a village. And why should people have to continue taking risks by nipping over the hedges with the law of indecent exposure being what it is?

Surrey Times

False teeth were thrown as 'confetti' at the Tynemouth wedding of dental surgeon Gordon Taylor of North Shields, and Miss Mary Smith of Tynemouth, yesterday. The teeth, not attached to plates, were collected by a guest from a dentist friend.

News of the World

Why is it that, in films, the hero never seems to get a trace of lipstick on him – even after the longest and most lingering kiss; yet my boyfriend always gets covered with it? As I have not had this trouble with previous boyfriends, should I change him?

Letter in *Woman's Own*

Where retirement causes panic

from DENNIS BLOODWORTH: Singapore, 11 Nov.

SINGAPORE is just emerging from a 12-day epidemic of fear.

It flashed through the Republic when it was rumoured that meat from pigs vaccinated against swine fever was spreading 'Koro', a marked retraction of the penis, which Chinese believe will vanish completely into the abdomen if unchecked, killing the victim.

All over the island desperate men, beset by a sudden

continued on page 47

This oversight on my part was caused by me filing the dividend warrant away among my personal effects and lying at the back of a wardrobe.

Letter from shareholder to company

● BABY boiler, good working order, £3.50

Advert in Shropshire paper

As at the last election, it has once again stuck to its old colours. (Loud cheers and cries of 'Good old True Gloucester (cheers and cries of 'Good old Glouloucester – (Cheers, and cries of 'ood old loucester').

Weekly paper

Meetings everywhere are crowded out. Not only that but luke-warm sympathizers are burning red-hot enthusiasts.

Clarion

Dame Flora returned 12 years later 'having screamed my way to the top' in a succession of classical and modern roles as outstanding neurotics. This time she arrived as leading lady and West Ham star.

Guardian

It is reported that the Foreign Secretary, who is undergoing treatment, has had a less restful night.

Swine fever has broken out.

Evening Standard

The marksmanship of the headquarters company is highly satisfactory and the shooting of the regimental sergeant-major was especially praiseworthy.

Daily Express

shrinking feeling, have abruptly exposed and seized their retiring natures, and then held them captive with chopsticks, a loop of wire, a bit of string or their bare hands while anxious bystanders have run for the doctor or dialled 999. At least 600 sufferers have hurried to hospitals and private clinics.

'Koro' was first mentioned in traditional Chinese medical treatises 3,000 years ago and has passed down in warning tones from generation to generation ever since. Senior medical experts here call it the 'cultural disease', since it is an inbuilt Chinese phobia. But it has also been found among Malaysian peoples and Sudanese, and both Indians and Malays have been among its victims this week.

Known as 'shookjong' by the local Chinese, 'Koro' seems to come from the Malay for tortoise and has no scientific Latin name. Western medicine regards it as a purely psychological affliction, an hysterical condition producing a real or imagined contraction of the male organ. But since anxiety can cause this shrinking, and the shrinking in turn causes anxiety, Singapore has been caught on a rising spiral of alarm.

Chinese healers have been curing cases with massage and herbal medicines (in one instance a mixture of pepper and brandy, half to be drunk, half to be rubbed into the affected part). Western-trained doctors have mainly talked the patient out of his panic. The ailing have been quickly cured.

Two successful press conferences by the Ministry of Culture have now cut the flow of 'Koro' cases to a trickle. But although the people of Singapore were told that the shrinkage was a harmless phenomenon and that pig vaccine and pork had nothing to do with it, many still clung to their old-fashioned fallacies. Slaughter in the abattoirs fell from about 1,300 pigs a day to 100.

Big business in any predominantly Chinese community, the pig trade collapsed. It is now very slowly reviving.

Observer

Recent animals at the Grand Hotel include Mr and Mrs Hayes.

Buenos Aires Herald

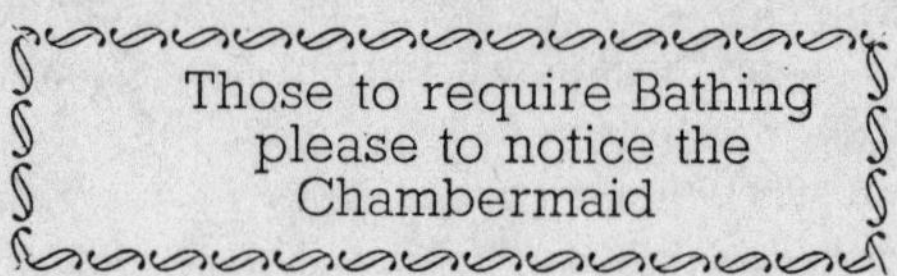

Notice in Spanish hotel

Earlier the same afternoon Mrs Jackson slipped off a bus and bruised a ship.

Uxbridge Weekly Post

He was taken to Wisbech's North Cambs Hospital with a broken nose and cuts. Expression of thanks to all who had contributed was made by the Vicar, Rev Gordon R—.

Wisbech Standard

DEAR MILKMAN, Baby arrived
yesterday, please leave another one.

Note to milkman

Rosmead was perfectly happy. He loved this woman with a great and growling love.

People's Friend

Francis Bellinghausen, of Stillwater, brother of the bride, was topped with a single white orchid.

Ponca City (Oklahoma) *News*

GIRL FOR TRIAL ON PRAWNS CHARGE

A 16-YEAR-OLD Scots girl is to go on trial in March charged with ill-treating prawns.

And the chief topic in the case at Duns Sheriff Court will be whether a prawn is a domestic animal, a fish in captivity, or neither.

The charge facing Eleanor Donoghy, of Springdale, Tweedmouth, Berwick, alleges she ill-treated the prawns – used in the processing of scampi – by putting them on a hot plate at an Eyemouth fish factory where she works.

When the girl made her first court appearance she admitted the offence. But after hearing part of the evidence from Procurator-fiscal Mr Hamish Stirling, Sheriff James Paterson stopped the case and told Donoghy to take legal advice.

Entering a plea of not guilty on her behalf in court today Mr Robert MacKay, solicitor, objected to the relevancy of the case on two grounds.

He claimed that the complaint must refer to animals. Under Section 13 of the 1912 Protection of Animals (Scotland) Act, animals was classed as any domestic or captive animal. Prawns were not mentioned.

Under another section, Mr MacKay pointed out that the Act referred to birds, fish and reptiles in captivity. If a prawn was, in fact, a fish he believed the word 'captivity' meant being kept alive in an aquarium.

But after referring to the standard natural history book, the solicitor emphasised that a prawn is not a fish.

The sheriff said he accepted if it was established a prawn was not a fish the prosecution would have grave difficulties in proceeding with the case.

He fixed trial for March 8.

Evening Express, Aberdeen

Kuida's skull was fractured and he was not given a chance to live by the attending physicians.

Ontario (California) *Daily Report*

FOR SALE. Three bra electric fire. Perfect £3.

Weekly Advertiser, Bristol

HUNT FOR BOY

ROAD BLOCKS were set up in five counties yesterday in a search for a boy who may have been abducted in Kendal, Westmoreland. A woman reported seeing a boy aged about 13 being forced into a small grey can on Sunday night by two men.

Guardian

STRADIVARIUS VIOLIN
FOR SALE CHEAP
Almost new

Advert in *All-Story Magazine*

Adjoining the kitchen department is the storeroom, containing a large refrigerator with separate compartments for meats, poultry, fish, and a small compartment for the household clerk.

Englishman

'Ever green' was Sir Joseph S—'s jocular reference to the new Lord Mayor and Lady Mayoress in his speech proposing the election of the Lord Mayor, and not 'very green', as given in our issue of yesterday.

Yorkshire Herald

Case of double glazing

A policeman said yesterday about a man accused of being drunk, 'He was unsteady on his feet, his breath smelt of alcohol and his eyes were glazed.' Hugh Jones, aged 40, a postal executive, removed his right eye and said: 'It was bound to be glazed.'

'The other one was glazed too,' Police Constable John Harris retorted. Mr Jones, who was conditionally discharged for three months at Thames Court for being drunk, replaced his eye before leaving court.

The Times

There is a spark of decency in every Englishman that makes him think that buying underwear is best left to women.

Letter in *Daily Mirror*

A friend of mine has her surname engraved on her upper set of false teeth. When she takes out her teeth, you can see her name clearly indented on the roof of her mouth.

Letter in *Reveille*

He was found not guilty of cruelly ill-treating a cat by cutting off its tail and beating it to death with a broom, but guilty of 'conduct to the prejudice of good order', in that he produced the severed tail to the airmen and airwomen in the dining-room.

Express and Echo, Exeter

Added Mrs Spragston, 'When Mrs Johns told me she had been intimate with my husband I refused to give her tea.'

Daily Express

It was Mr Wilson's use of the wrods 'in due course' which inserted the extra qualith of e uivocation. As soon as he uttered them the Conservative benches let out a concerted 'Ah'.

Guardian

The large comet was seen by a resident in the heavens in the direction of the Forest.

Football Echo

On several occasions the thick end of the divining rod rose up and struck the operator on the head. On these spots, he asserted, water would be found fifty feet down.

Daily Mirror

THE QUEEN TO BE SOLD BIT BY BIT

Headline in *Australian*

All those who wish to give eggs to the needy are asked to lay them in the font.

Parish magazine

Instant hot water
in five minutes

Notice in York boarding-house

Sir, Mr Scrimgeour (Business News, June 29) may be interested to know that the scientific aspects of the manufacture and use of the British sausage have been investigated in these laboratories since 1926 and one of the topics which was investigated was the science of sausage pricking.

The alleged objective of sausage pricking was the prevention of sausages from bursting their bounds on frying. The conclusion reached was that one need only fry them gently and pricking was quite unnecessary.

It is as well that this was the conclusion since the experiments were abruptly terminated when the 'standard fork' used for pricking was inadvertently used as a can opener and its dimensions altered.

Yours etc, A. W. Holmes, Director, British Food Manufacturing Industries Research Association.

The Times

Two men arrested for trying to buy gold from a supposed black-marketeer, who turned out to be a police inspector, have been released after proving that they too were police inspectors, masquerading as black-market operators.

Edinburgh Evening Dispatch

Sir, The other morning, boarding a Metropolitan train at Kings Cross a woman watched her ball of wool fall from her bag and out through the closing sliding doors. I would have cut my losses but she, clutching her knitting, steadily hauled in the trailing wool. By the time Euston was reached, egged on by admiring fellow passengers, she had retrieved all the wool. Is this a record?

Yours faithfully,

Letter in *The Times*

For some informality in front of the Durham goal posts, Gamon had a free kick allowed, but he made a wretched attempt with him to shake hands and say good-bye, for he was later.

Yorkshire Post

The Transvaal team for the match against Western Province today will not, it is stated, be chosen until tomorrow morning.

Rand Daily Mail

 **Children's heads neatly executed** 

Notice in picture gallery

For those who like watching trains, as I occasionally do, the express passes through a halt a couple of miles away. And there are fishermen by the canal, running alongside the railway, willing to talk about pike.

from *Wiltshire Harvest* by H. H. Bashford

High as the goal-bar this effort came skimming along, with every eye of the vast throng watching its progress on tiptoe.

Glasgow News

Captain Rogers shot a pariah dog in the grounds of the Terrace a few days ago and was destroyed in the bazaar the following morning.

Pioneer

Young lady would like talkative Parrot for company; parents recently died; must be cheap.

Advert in *Bristol Evening Post*

Puddle muddle

A man caught picking up winkles from a puddle on a mudflat landed in court. His lawyer argued that winkles could not reasonably be called 'fish', but the judge replied that oysters had been called such by another judge, and that winkles were in the same category.

The lawyer tried a different angle by pleading that even if winkles were 'fish' a puddle could not be regarded as 'private water'. The judge disagreed and said that as puddles normally contain water, and as the puddle was on private land, it was private water. The winkle stealer was found guilty and fined.

Reveille

Traveller who has to cover his ground by train needs one or two large coffins to take evening dresses, must be strong and able to lock.

Advert in *Nottingham Evening News*

Mr George H—, 22, the new president of the Oxford Union, worked as a navvy for a short time before going up to Oxford. In some editions on Saturday, owing to a mishearing on the telephone, it was stated that he was a former Nazi. The mistake is much regretted.

Daily Telegraph

LONELY LADY, 43, with little dog, seeks post.

Exeter Express and Echo

THE DAFFODIL BALL – By a misprint this ball was stated to have been organized by the National Society of Cruelty to Animals. It should, of course, have been children not animals.

Irish Independent

Dr Garside said that after the accident Williams did several of the tests quite well. Williams told him he had been to a very good dinner and had a good deal to drink at it. He was certain that his car had touched nothing.

Bristol Evening Post

Chairman of the Bench, Mr A. C. Bailey, told him: 'You are now living in England, and we would like you to forget this and live a decent and ordered life in the future.'

Nelson Leader

SIAMESE KITTENS, very good points and eyes; dam good pedigree.

Advert in local paper

The doctor's and his wife, it was stated today, were often seen riding in a car which plunged 300 feet into the sea off Beachy Head.

Evening News

My little boy (aged seven) has a passion for dogs, and swears that when he is a man he will have ten sons; that he will give each of them a dog; and that they shall all – dogs and sons – sleep in hammocks.

It seems to me it will be very uncomfortable for his wife. Can I do anything to correct this tendency?

Letter in the *People*

Two men were brushing snow from the road into the gutter. They were followed by two more, shovelling snow from the gutter onto the road. Overcome by curiosity a bystander enquired the reason for this strange lack of coordination.

From the first sweeper came the reply, 'Oh, the other two are town men. We come under the County.'

Cornish Echo, quoted in *New Statesman*'s 'This England'

The snail watchers are interested in snails from all angles. They search literature and art for references. At the moment they are investigating the snail's reaction to music. 'We have played to them on the harp in the garden and in the country on the pipe', said Mr Heaton, 'and we have taken them into the house and played to them on the piano.'

quoted in *New Statesman*'s 'This England'

At the end of January people near Scarborough were claiming to have heard the first cuckoo. But this week Mr Hezekiah Johnson, a corporation road cleaner, said: 'I wait until a crowd gathers at the bus stop and then I go into the park nearby and do the cuckoo. They all take it in.' He added: 'I used to do the nightingale when I had my teeth in.'

Evening Standard

The announcement that the Vicar has raided a fund for the support of the unfortunate man's wife will be welcomed by all.

Derby paper

The appeal of Morris Hindle against removal from the register was dismissed. Hindle is a painter and decorator, and part-time Jehovah's fish-retailer, Kendal.

Guardian

Dr Cook's telegram to M Lecointe states definitely that he reached the North Pole on the date mentioned above, and that he discovered land to the northward.

Daily Telegraph

The bridesmaids, both sisters of the bride, wore dresses of lavender and blue net respectively, with head-dresses and mittens to tone. Both carried Victorian Derek Bates brother of the bridegroom.

Penrith Oberver

ARMY OFFICER FIRES TOY PISTOL

Fined for Dangerous Driving

Khartoum Morning News

Melt the butter in a frying pan. When frothing, pour in the egg mixture and immediately lower the heat.

The Times

This is a good teaching film. No high or low church bias . . . that is left for the teacher to put in.

Religious films catalogue

NOTE TO EMPLOYER

It is regretted that it was not possible to send the enclosed forms to you before the date by which, had you received them, you would be required to forward completed copies to this Office.

Government form

It was at the Algonquin Hotel, with its lively literary associations, that we settled the plural form of shrimp. Speaking of fish, one shrimp is a shirmp, and 1000 shirmp are shrimp; it's only the human kind that take an 's' in the plural. A dried-up little man is a shrimp: two of him are shirmps.

Chicago Tribune

March 22nd: For Sale. Slightly used farm wench in good condition. Very handy. Phone 336–R–2. A. Cartright.

March 29th: Correction. Due to an unfortunate error, Mr Cartright's ad last week was not clear. He has an excellent winch for sale. We trust this will put an end to jokesters who have called Mr Cartright and greatly bothered his housekeeper, Mrs Hargreaves, who loves with him.

April 9th: Notice! My WINCH is not for sale. I put a sledgehammer to it. Don't bother calling 336–R–2. I had the phone taken out. I am not carrying on with Mrs Hargreaves. She merely LIVES here. A. Cartright.

Connecticut paper quoted in *Readers' Digest*

By that simple and dishonest device, he forced the British to reopen talks they had concluded. Sir Alec, like Harold Wilson after him, was to scratch his head at the anticssbfszyus strange man who dusbfe thing andszbwd the world Prtss he wassdoing the the oppposite.

Australasian

Time and again the Scots found space down the left. Hughes was not a great deal more reassuring, his lack of a left foot again being apparent.

Sunday Times

The coffee house will have the services of two efficient 'captains' and twelve polite and courteous waitresses, specially selected for their experiences, to attend to customers.

Straits Times

FOR SALE. Three-piece suite.
Settee turns into bed covered in thick
yellow mustard.

Midlands paper

Brian Saunders has been awarded the RSPCA bronze medal for rescuing a car trapped up a tree.

Berkshire paper

The Rev R. B. Tanner said: 'I was rather disappointed. We know he has a little bee in his belfry. Now he has got it off his chest I hoped there would be something this time about the spread of dysentery.'

Eastern Daily Press

Sir, When I was a judo instructor I always used to ask trainees to stand on their heads at the first interview. Those who swayed towards the left ear were nearly always women, and those who swayed towards the right ear, nearly always men. The test was 99 per cent infallible. Yours etc.

Letter in *Observer*

Einstein theory led to arson

Because he disagreed with Einstein's theory of relativity Michael Victor Dobson, aged 27, went to Harrow School and set fire to and destroyed a shed, the prosecution said at Middlesex Area Sessions yesterday. Damage was estimated at £796. Mr Dobson, unemployed, of Aberdeen Road, Wealdstone, Middlesex, pleaded guilty to a charge of arson.

The Times

Miklos Levay, soaked to the skin, thumbed a lift from a lorry on the road between Balmazujvaros and Budapest in Hungary. In the back was an empty coffin. Levay climbed in and closed the lid.

Further down the road the lorry stopped again and another hitch-hiker climbed aboard. Later, when the rain stopped, Levay felt hot and stuffy inside the coffin. So he raised the lid and shouted, 'What's the weather like?'

His fellow hitch-hiker screamed with fear, jumped off the fast-moving truck in panic, broke a leg and suffered various other injuries. Later he took Levay and the driver, Janos Mihaly, to court, charging them with grievous bodily harm.

But the judge dismissed the case. He told the court, 'Surely any adult knows perfectly well that the dead cannot rise from their coffins. In any case, there is no rule that I am aware of which states that every coffin must contain a dead body.'

Weekend

SIGNALMAN MISSING BY MISTAKE

PASSENGERS DIVERTED

Scotsman

Evidence was given by PC Hart who described how he saw wrapping and later roll it into Smith eating from a paper a ball and throw it on the street.

Gloucester Citizen

Among the special attractions especial interest was aroused by the offer of very reduced princes in the hotels for stays at Sorrento.

Travel brochure

The reception in the Oddfellows' Hall, Hinstock, was attended by about 50 guests. For the honeymoon at Torquay the bride travelled in a camel.

Market Drayton Advertiser

WELSH PUBLIC BODIES
GET CIRCULAR

Western Morning News

Dr Addison, who is a leading authority on this important subject, will speak on the general questions of weed control and Miss Thompson will follow with a short talk on the control of wild oats of which she has made a special study.

A committee notice

The librarian at the Building Research Station was somewhat puzzled by the demand for old copies of the *Daily Telegraph*. This too from the plumbing section, who seemed to be showing unexpected interest in right-wing politics. It emerged eventually that the standard test of a good flush is the ability to swallow half a *Daily Telegraph*.

New Scientist

HIS LORDSHIP: I suppose the word 'horse' in the rule does not include an aeroplane?
COUNSEL: No, I think not.
HIS LORDSHIP: It ought to, it is much the same thing.
COUNSEL: I think that it was put in for the relief of the archdeacon.

The Times Law Report

TOILETS OUT OF ORDER
Use platforms 3-4, 7-8

Sign at New South Wales station

Sir, Recently we witnessed a 50p coin, tossed for the usual reason that one tosses a coin, land on its edge and remain so standing. We should like to record this realization of an event traditionally accorded a probability of zero.
We are, yours faithfully,
SUSAN M. CHAMBERS
PETER McLEOD
BRYAN J. T. MORGAN
MRC Applied Psychology Unit, 15 Chaucer Road, Cambridge

Letter in *The Times*

'DON'T PRINT THE STORY OF MY TRIAL,' SHE SOBS

Full amazing story – Page 10.

Sunday Mail, Scotland

His secretary and right-hand-man 53-year-old Polycarpos Ioannides was inspecting a half-finished building with his arms folded behind him in a nearby street. Suddenly both were seized and flown to Nicosia by helicopter.

Daily Sketch

Mrs Elizabeth Smith (Chairman) gave a talk on Spain, including a description of a bullfight at the luncheon meeting of Cowplain and Waterlooville Ladies Club.

Portsmouth and Southsea Evening News

In view of the high proportion of children who are receiving a good balanced midday meal in the secondary schools it is debatable whether there is much to be gained by also providing mink in these schools.

Liverpool Daily Post

Very easily run business, travelling lending library latest books, late type van, good rounds, good loving assured, suit woman . . .

London Weekly Advertiser

The raider brandished a gin as he entered the bank.

Denver Post

Naked jungle (film) Lovely young widow Eleanor Parker finds life with her husband almost impossible on a plantation, until a plague of advancing ants brings a turn for the better.

What's On In London

One John Kidely threw four small Fishes into the House; when Elizabeth Dunn, a Neighbour, took up one of them (a Perch) and, by squeezing, endeavoured to kill it. Thomas Butlin told Dunn that if she did it again he would put it in her mouth.

She opened her mouth and the Fish at the same Instant springing from Butlin's Hand into her Throat (where it remained immoveable) caused her immediate Death.

Northampton Mercury, 1780

A Londonderry businessman who reproached his estate agent for repeatedly misspelling his name in correspondence has now received a letter saying: 'Please state reasons for change of name.'

Peterborough in *Daily Telegraph*

Man barks at dog, fined £5

Mr Claude Wilson, aged 34, of Benfleet, Essex, a teacher, who barked at an Alsatian after it barked at him, and had a scuffle with its owner, was fined £5 with £5 costs by Rochford magistrates yesterday.

The Times

Police apologized for the non-appearance of a minced-beef pie in a shoplifting case before magistrates at Heanor, Derbyshire yesterday. It had been eaten by mistake, said the prosecutor, Mr John Caslon. *Evening News*

The girls wore transparent pink robes split at the waist, a cluster of young split at the waist, a cluster of young g-o split at the waist, a cluster of young goddesses with perspiration on their faces.

Vancouver Daily Province

Tonight as a verger stoked the great stoves in the gloom of Chester's medieval cathedral preparations were being made to hold the trail of the Rev Philip Roberts in a tiny chamber separated from the knave by a grille of open stonework.

Daily Mail

Tripoli, Saturday. The government committee for locusts are invading Libya and the country may in four months be facing one of the biggest invasions on record.

Times of Cyprus

Two days later a woman walked into the Wigan Borough Police Station, thumped a large parcel on the information room desk and told them the contents were the old men mentioned in the Evening Chronicle.

Manchester Evening Chronicle

Ducking under crossing gates and running behind a westbound freight train, an electric passenger train which he was trying to catch struck and mangled Henry Rasku of 122 Lockman Avenue today.

Evening Post, USA

Returning he wonders if he will make it in time for the Hore of the Year Show on Colour TV.

Evening Herald, Dublin

Reporter Wendy Henry, 21, crashed her car into an articulated lorry which had jack-knifed on the A57 Sheffield to Manchester road. She was rushed to hospital with a fractured wrist, broken nose and cuts on face and leg.

But Wendy, who works with Manchester News Service, was back at work even before she got into the operating theatre. While the doctors were studying her X-rays, she noticed someone else's X-ray plates clearly showing that the person had swallowed a 50p piece.

So, while Wendy was waiting for her operation, she persuaded a nurse to bring the coin swallower to her bedside. Then she got the nurse to write the story while she interviewed him. He told Wendy he had been balancing the coin on the end of his nose to amuse his niece, who nudged him and caused the accident.

UK Press Gazette

ENGINEER FIRED IN CANNON

A WELDING ENGINEER was accidentally fired from a funfair cannon at Queniborough, Leicestershire, yesterday but escaped with minor injuries to his back and legs.

Mr Tom Pretty, 44, was head-first half-way down the barrel of a 16ft cannon, trying to adjust its range, when the explosive charge went off. He was hurled over a wall and 50 feet into a field.

The accident led the human cannonball, Mr Fred Frinton, 42, who is usually fired from the gun to threaten strike action. He is due to be 'fired' at Woolston Park, Nottingham, tomorrow, but he said, 'Unless I get an assurance that a skilled technician has corrected the fault I shall not appear this weekend.'

Daily Telegraph

I thought there had been a power-cut. Next smoke was pouring out. Within minutes there was a smell of burning and thick firemen had removed the set.

Newham Recorder

The County Surveyor proposes to put down white lies to indicate that Main Road/Windsor Road is a continuous route.

Peterborough Evening Telegraph

There will also be a demonstration of composting underground to High Barnet, and then 107 or 306 bus to Arkley war memorial.

Methodist Recorder

Three old men sat on the wench, munching sandwiches.

Weekly News, New Zealand

However, my mother, who has not heard about contact lenses before, is strongly against the idea of wearing them and has found out that contact lenses may not be suitable for everyone. Can any obstetrician enlighten me on this matter?

Straits Times, Singapore

Save for the holidays. Put your savings into the GREENOCK PROVIDENT BANK Ladies – Corsets Back Lacing, Front Lacing. Underbelts. Busk Wraps and Hookside.

Greenock Telegraph

Detectives kept a witch on the house for two weeks.

Clapham Observer

On his first – and last – assignment for a local newspaper in Chicago, a reporter drove the firm's car to a car-crashing plant, parked in the wrong place and returned from interviewing the manager in time to see the vehicle being squashed into scrap metal.

Tit-Bits

When asked what changes we could expect by the year 2000, a French scientist pondered, then replied. 'Well, Brigitte Bardot will be 65.'

Peterborough in *Daily Telegraph*

Getting in on the act

Have you ever been puzzled by the difference between an Extra and a Walk-on? Perhaps not, but people at the BBC evidently have, for a memo has just been sent round to enlighten them. It cites the following examples:

1 A 'policeman' standing at the corner of a street, alone, but not doing anything in particular, would be an Extra. If he was called upon to do anything specific to the action of the drama he becomes a Walk-on I; if he speaks he is a Walk-on II.

2 A 'barman' seen in long-shot busying himself in normal barman work would be an Extra; if he serves a pint to a leading character on cue he becomes a Walk-on I; if he speaks a few unimportant words, he becomes a Walk-on II.

3 A 'gardener' alone in a long-shot sweeping a drive would be an Extra; if he is seen in close-up grimacing, he becomes a Walk-on I.

So the next time you see a grimacing gardener in close-up on BBC Television, please remember his proper title.

Financial Times

Lady required for 6 hours per week to clean small officers at Station Road, Witney.

Witney and West Oxfordshire Gazette

Application forms and £1,925 may be obtained from the County Librarian, County Hall.

Evening Argus, Brighton

A very useful service is offered by GARDEN CULTIVATION LTD. They will turn a garden into a wilderness under the expert supervision of Mr David French.

Evening Gazette, Middlesbrough

FOR SALE, two office desks, one Executive Chair and one typit's hair.

Local paper

'What upset me was to have this girl described in detail, even her public hair.'

News of the World

There is a fantastic range of stereo equipment and a choice of around 3,000 musical apes which is enough to make any music lover stop in his tracks for a second look.

Colchester Express

SWAP HUSBAND and duplex flat near Peninsula Hotel for accommodation with garden. Please reply to Box 1314.

Advert in *Hong Kong China Mail*

An Irish football club secretary entrusted his wife with the job of getting a presentation tankard engraved; the inscription was to read, 'To Mr M. P. Clark in appreciation for the Whitsun 1974 tour', and this much duly appeared on the tankard's side. Unfortunately, as the words had been written out on a shopping list, the message went on: 'One bottle of shoe cleaner and a pair of white laces.'

World Medicine

The explanation given by Patrick Rivers to the police for a dead but still warm pheasant found in the lining of his jacket was that he had seen the bird walking down the road looking poorly and he felt sorry for it.

Leicester Mercury

A HONEYMOON couple quarrelled – and the husband threw his wedding ring over a railway bridge. Then they kissed and made up – and asked the manager at New Street railway station, Birmingham, to help them find the ring.

But it was somewhere on one of the busiest lines in the country. Operating assistants got the husband to throw a bottle top from the bridge, watched it land, and found the ring only a yard away.

Daily Mail

Family Planning Clinic, Westfield Walk, Leominster. First and third Thursday in every month. Turf supplied.

Leominster News

NEW SULTAN OF MOROCCO ENTITLED TO FOUR WIVES: PREFERS MAHOGANY

Omaha Bee-News

There were about six customers on the forecourt at the time of the raid – about 11.30 a.m. – and thieves and anybody else with information should contact police.

Southern Evening Echo

A total of 15,520 students have been attached to pillars at Victoria shopping centre, Nottingham, to help blind customers find their way round.

Daily Telegraph

JURY TO TRY WOMAN FOR MURDER NOT YET COMPLETED

Ithaca (N.Y.) *Journal-News*

For my own part I have been cleaning orchards and truck patches and clearing out old blackberry patches and trying to get he hens to lay.

Coffeyville (Kansas) *Gazette*

Hungarian science student Hans Panek has claimed a national record for rolling an egg over a five-mile course, without cracking it, in 11 hours 16 minutes.

Weekend

YOU ARE familiar with the whole story: here is the story with a hole in it.

A freelance photographer put a parcel on a train to Waterloo. The parcel was lost and a national newspaper picture desk spent four hours begging, pleading and threatening in an effort to locate it.

Eventually it was found and rushed triumphantly to the office. When the package was opened, the picture desk found – wrapped inside the photographer's caption – one roll of Polo mints.

When informed of this by phone, one very embarrassed photographer felt in his top pocket, and dashed off to bring the roll of film to Fleet Street by car. And, of course, to collect his mints.

UK Press Gazette

NEW POISON THREAT
AS MINISTER
HEADS FOR BEACHES

Headline in *Evening Standard*

But change is on the way. When it comes, we shall, alas, lose that famous line in the Irish Customs regulations – 'Forbidden imports: After contraceptives, insert fresh fruit and vegetables.'

Literary weekly

A man we know also saw the strange figure and it upset him so much that he has not eaten property for some days.

Sheffield Star

CORONER FINDS DRIVER HAD TAKEN ONLY FOUR LESSONS BEFORE HITTING CAR.

Connecticut News

Gunalan was deadly on his smashes from the back of the court and kept Ghosh guessing by mixing in some delightful drop shorts.

Anrita Bazar Patrika, Calcutta

● 10.0 – NEWS AT TEN (With Anne Howard, John Hauxwell, Arthur Blake and his orchestra.)

Evening Citizen, Glasgow

FAMILY PLUMBING. Write or call for price list. Rotherham Surgical Co, 71 Effingham St.

Advert in *Sheffield Telegraph*

Guest celebrity at next year's Festival of Music will be John Betjeman, poet and worshipper, of Victoriana.

Music journal

BIG PETWORTH WIN FOR QUEEN
Major show success
for Windsor cow

The News, Portsmouth

Simon Short's Son Samuel

The following literary curiosity was constructed for the last number of the Aspirant, the reading of which formed a part of the closing exercises of the Concord, N. H., High school. The writer is Miss Ida Bennett:

Shrewd Simon Short sewed shoes. Seventeen summers, speeding storms, spreading sunshine successively, saw Simon's small, shabby shop, still standing staunch, saw Simon's self-same squeaking sign still swinging silently specifying:

Simon Short, Smithfield's sole surviving shoemaker. Shoes sewed soled superfinely.

Simon's spry, sedulous, spouse, Sally Short, sewed skirts, stitched sheets, stuffed sofas. Simon's six stout sons – Seth, Samuel, Stephen, Saul, Silas, Shadrach – sold sundries. Sober Seth sold sugar, spices; simple Sam sold saddles, stirrups, screws; sagacious Stephen sold silks, satins, shawls; skeptical Saul sold silver salvers; selfish Shadrach sold salves, shoe strings, soap, saws, skates; slack Silas sold Sally Short's stuffed sofas.

Some seven summers since, Simon's second son Samuel saw Sophia Sophronia Spriggs somewhere. Sweet, smart, sensible Sophia Sophronia Spriggs. Sam soon showed strong symptoms. Sam seldom stayed storing, selling saddles. Sam sighed sorrowfully, sought Sophia Sophronia's society, sung several serenades slyly. Simon stormed, scolded severely, said Sam seemed so silly singing such shameful, senseless songs. 'Strange Sam should slight such splendid sales! Strutting spendthrift! Shattered-brained simpleton.'

'Softly, softly, sire,' said Sally. – 'Sam's smitten; Sam's spied some sweetheart.'

'Sentimental school-boy!' snarled Simon. 'Smitten! Stop such stuff.' Simon sent Sally's snuff-box spinning, seized Sally's scissors, smashed Sally's spectacles, scattering several spools. 'Sneaking scoundrel! Sam's shocking silliness shall surcease!' Scowling, Simon stopped speaking, started swiftly shopward. Sally sighed sadly. Summoning Sam, she spoke sweet sympathy. 'Sam,' said she, 'sire seems singularly snappy; so, solicit, sue, secure Sophronia speedily, Sam.'

'So soon? so soon?' said Sam, standing stock still.

'So soon, surely,' said Sally smilingly, 'specially since sire shows such spirits.'

So Sam somewhat scared, sauntered slowly, shaking stupendously. Sam soliloquises: 'Sophia Sophronia Spriggs, Spriggs – Short – Sophia Sophronia Short – Samuel Short's spouse – sounds splendid! Suppose she should say – she shan't – she shan't!'

Soon Sam spied Sophia starching shirts, singing softly. Seeing Sam she stopped starching, saluting Sam smilingly. Sam stammered shockingly.

'Spl-spl-splendid summer season, Sophia.'

'Selling saddles still, Sam?'

'Sar-sar-tin,' said Sam, starting suddenly. 'Season's somewhat sudorific,' said Sam, steadily, staunching streaming sweat, shaking sensibly.

'Sartin,' said Sophia, smiling significantly. 'Sip some sweet sherbit, Sam.' (Silence sixty seconds.)

'Sire shot sixty shelldrakes, Saturday,' said Sophia.

'Sixty? sho!' said Sam. (Silence seventy-seven seconds.)

'See sister Susan's sunflowers,' said Sophia socially, silencing such stiff silence.

Sophia's sprightly sauciness stimulated Sam strangely; so Sam suddenly spoke sentimentally; 'Sophia, Susan's sunflowers seem saying Samuel Short, Sophia Sophronia Spriggs, stroll serenely, seek some sequestered spot, some sylvan shade. Sparkling springs shall sing soul-stirring strains; sweet songsters shall silence secret sighings; superangelic sylphs shall' – Sophia snickered; so Sam stopped.

continued

'Sophia,' said Sam solemnly.

'Sam,' said Sophia.

'Sophia, stop smiling; Sam Short's sincere. Sam's seeking some sweet spouse, Sophia.'

Sophia stood silent.

'Speak Sophia, speak; such suspense speculates sorrow.'

'Seek sire, Sam, seek sire.'

So Sam sought sire Spriggs, sire Spriggs said 'Sartin.'

Middlebury (Vermont) *Register*

Some of the world's top expectorators congregated recently for the 9th annual Tobacco Chewin' and Spittin' Championships. The expectorators – spitters – came from all over America to St Louis, Missouri, to pit their skill in the various events.

There was the distance competition, which was won by a cowboy from Texas (of course) with a new record spit of 18ft 3½in, with no wind assistance. The accuracy event went to a Chicago billiards hall attendant who hit a small thimble from 10 ft.

The speed title, for rapid-fire spitting at a moving target, was won by a 63-year-old farmer from North Dakota who peppered the target for 60 seconds.

Weekend

HAVING resigned after two years as a Civil Service typist, I was awaiting a letter to tell me my notice had been accepted. I was annoyed, therefore, when this very letter was given me to type. I received it two days later, complete with my initials, thanking me for my services.

Miss E. Marshall, Walthamstow

Letter in *Sunday Mirror*

Professor Semple said re-heating did not destroy germs which were likely to be on food after being handled, especially by someone with a scratch or cut on their hands. Germans, too, could be found lurking on wall can-openers. Such openers ought to be kept scrupulously clean, he advised.

Liverpool Echo and Evening Express

RICHARD BURTON, who plays the lead, and Elizabeth Taylor (who doesn't) arrived in Mexico City to be greeted by 1,500 screaming fans. With them were Lisa Todd, Miss Taylor's daughter by the late Mike Todd and several assistants.

Daily Mail

Let Liverpool – the first city to appoint a Medical Officer of Health – again give a national lead to other great cities by fluoridating her water, and let the slogan be 'What Liverpool drinks today – the rest of the country drinks tomorrow.'

Liverpool Echo

BRIDES-TO-BE. Your trousseau require 12-bore L. Franchi shotgun, over and under, as new, $360.

Rhodesia Herald

AUSTIN 1100 1967, 24,000 miles, service certificate, lady under radio, extras, £485.

Advert in *Southern Evening Echo*

FLUSH OUT OF CASH

MR OLIVER STARK asked a workmate to take his pay home to Mrs Stark yesterday. The man called at the Stark house in Surrey Rd, South Yarra, but Mrs Stark was not at home.

He slipped the pay packet through a louvre window. It fell into the lavatory bowl. Young Christopher Stark came home with his mother and went to the lavatory. He flushed the packet away.

Sun, Australia

SYDNEY The 8.28 train pulled out from Westmead station on time last night, bound for Central. It carried the $95 takings from the Westmead station about 15 miles west of the city. The money was handed over to a guard by station assistant Eric Foster.

A minute later two armed men entered the ticket office and demanded the takings. Foster told them, 'You have missed out. The money's on the train.' Said one gunman, 'Just our luck. The train's usually bloody late.'

Sydney Morning Herald

Farmworker's wife Mrs Josephine Chapman claimed that the estranged wife of her next-door neighbour did not wear knickers when she and her husband visited them.

So, it was alleged at the Old Bailey today, she set fire to their house.

Evening News

PREGNANT WOMAN BITES PC

Headline in *Epping and Ongar Gazette*

Dr L. seeks small cottage property in St Albans or surrounding village with 2 bedrooms and 22 reception rooms. Condition immaterial.

Herts Advertiser

There will be 'zero gravity' toilets which advise passengers to read the instructions before use, and colour television in every seat.

Wimbledon News

Birthday memories of a dear husband and father, Frank, died October 14th 1966.

From his loving wife Mary, son George and daughter etc. APPLY ANY EVENING AFTER Susan.

Burnley Evening Star

Prior to his return to work this morning he spent the weekend at his fiancée's home and is now back on the job better versed in business methods.

Connecticut paper

She used an ordinary casting rod and light tickle.

Freeport (Illinois) *News*

Out to lunch.
If not back by five
out to dinner also.

Notice on Ealing shop door

Sir, Honda way to the office each day in my all British (?) Ford, I am cortina ever increasing flow of foreign cars and cannot help wondering what is the mazda with the home car industry. The overseas manufacturers have us at their mercedes days and datsun obvious statement of fact.

Our only opel be to have a thorough peugeot our production methods and toyota get on with it straight away. This is no time for citroen on their backsides, audi will be renault of business!

Yours fiat-fully, A. FIDLER, Wirral

Letter to *The Times*

Getting the goods was an embarrassment for Mr Joseph Begley, of Evesham, Worcestershire. He sent 2,000 coupons to a cigarette company and ordered a watch. None arrived, so he wrote to tell them. The company then sent three watches and Mr Begley returned two.

In the next two days 28 parcels from the tobacco people arrived. Among them, three tape recorders, a doll, a golf bag, two electric blankets, a cot, saucepans, a pressure cooker and some records.

Mr B. returned them and the company sent him 10,000 coupons to compensate him for his trouble. With them he ordered tools and a bedspread. No messing about this time. Almost by return he was sent a plant stand and two stepladders.

Weekend

INSTRUCTIONS Besmear a backing-pan, previously buttered with a good tomato sauce and after, dispose the Canelloni, lightly distanced between them in a only couch.

Instructions on packet

Joe Stenosklaip, of Streator, has just received a letter from his wife in Italy telling of the birth of a son. Joe immediately set the boys up to drinks, and stated that he had not seen his wife for five years.

Washburn (Illinois) *Leader*

FOR SALE, motor bike, suit 34 bust.

Advert in local paper

I, Arthur Brown, 28 Mead Street, Mackay, did not on the 25th April wear anything but war medals. Persons spreading reports otherwise will be prosecuted.

Daily Mercury

PERSONAL

Nabil, come home, your mother forgives you and your brother is going to be president of the Badminton Club – Your fiancée, Tu-tu.

Advert in *Outlook* (American University of Beirut)

The present session got off to a 'sizzling' start with a barbecue, complete with soup, sausages and some of the older Saturday Club members.

Northern Ireland parish magazine

Ex-alderman dies
ONE OF EIGHT AXED
BY TORIES

Coventry Evening Telegraph

The postal service is often criticized, but back in 1916 the American parcel post system saved a building contractor a lot of money. The contractor had to build a bank in Utah but the nearest brickworks was 400 miles away. And hauliers wanted 5p a brick to deliver them to the site.

The contractor realized the parcel post rate up to 50 lb was cheaper, so he arranged for the brickworks to post the bricks in parcels of 10.

The authorities soon found that all the bricks were clogging up the mails and invoked an old regulation preventing more than 200 lb of mail being delivered to any address in one day. But the contractor sidestepped that one by getting the bricks sent in small consignments to his employees. Then he collected them and the bank was finished on time – and cheaper.

Weekend

ROME, Tuesday

CARMELO PERINO, 24, objected to being stopped for speeding yesterday. So he shot the policeman. Then he drove off to find another officer who prosecuted him for careless driving a year ago, found the man at home with his wife, and killed them both.

Daily Mail

NEW YORK 'Sometimes I think they would give these credit cards to a dog,' Donald Boyd, a motor company treasurer, said to his wife when yet another application form turned up in his mail. Mrs Boyd didn't agree. So her husband filled in the form for Tarreytown, their Dalmatian. It ran: Age 2.7 years; occupation, watchdog; income, nil. Back by return of post came Tarreytown's credit card for a department store in Troy, Michigan. Since then the dog has received a circular describing him as a 'preferred customer.'

Daily Express

PROBATION

At Frome yesterday Mrs Jennifer Ann Green of Kean Street, Frome, was placed on probation for three years for stealing the Gas Board.

Bath Evening Chronicle

LIVESTOCK FOR SALE – Pedigree Mare, in perfect condition, hard body, fold away base. What offers?

Drogheda Independent

Negro singer Gereros Dorsetta has refused to give any evidence to New York police about the night-club shooting which resulted in Billy Daniels, the coloured singer, being charged with assault and carrying a gnu.

Daily Mail

Palace are hoping Milligan will be fat enough to play.

Croydon Advertiser

Although he was represented by a solicitor, Beamish said that he wanted to address the magistrate himself. He said: 'I really do want to make a fresh tart. I am fond of the country and would be perfectly happy working at the bird sanctuary.'

Irish Times

PC Watkins told me that he keeps Hobo at home at night and that the dog leads a life just like any other domestic criminal.

Wembley Observer and Gazette

Greater role seen for rape

WINNIPEG A University of Manitoba research specialist who has been studying rapeseed for the last 17 years says the plant...

Canadian paper

Councillor Eric Hendrie drew attention to an item in the report which he said gave him considerable concern. This was that pigs had been seen to panic and run down a slope into a scalding tank. What concerned him was that if this could happen to pigs it could happen to the attendants.

Scotsman

In one day in June 1959 a female elephant in a Dutch zoo was offered and ate: 1,706 peanuts, 1,330 sweets, 981 pieces of bread, 811 sugared biscuits, 198 sandwiches, 188 pieces of orange, 13 pieces of paper, 5 ice-creams, 3 paper bags, a hamburger, a boot lace and a white glove. The total weight was about 128 lb.

Reveille

Zurich, Aug 20 A Swiss couple who went on holiday to Hong Kong have returned without their poodle Rosa after a traumatic experience in a Chinese restaurant.

They told the newspaper *Blick* that they asked a waiter over to their table and pointed to the poodle while they made eating motions to show they wanted it to be fed.

Eventually the waiter appeared to understand and took Rosa off into the kitchen. About an hour later he came back with their main dish and when they picked up the silver lid they found their poodle roasted inside, garnished with pepper, sauce and bamboo shoots. The couple, suffering from emotional shock, decided to return to Zurich immediately.

The Times (by permission)

But Foster showed he has a magnificent left jab as well, and several times all 79 inches of his lean left arm slammed into Finnegan's face.

Sun

Smorgasbord with Rolls and Butter and a Carafino of Wind – all for £1 – has proved infinitely popular.

Evening Post, Reading

South African-born Miss Virginia Rossouw, who now lives at Ashurst Wood, has added yet another beauty title to her collection – the fourth this year. Last week she was chosen 'The Prettiest Girl in a Bathing Costume' at the Broadstairs water gala. Miss Rossouw went to collect her prize alongside Opposition Leader Mr Edward Heath, who finished second.

Westerham Courier

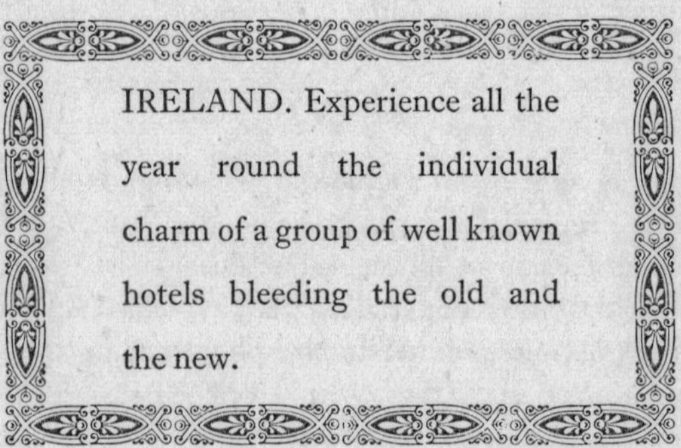

Advert in the *Observer*

☞ **Wheel changing.** The square wheel is located below the luggage compartment.

1970 Simca 1100 driver's handbook

WOULD ANY surviving ancestors of Fred Nerde
(Drake's cabin boy) please contact
Box 1939F, The Times.

Advert in *The Times*

Note to schoolteacher: 'Please don't force Sheila to take her helping of cabbage at school meals. She just brings it home every day stuffed down her socks.'

quoted in *Tit-Bits*

The management has decided to introduce a more efficient and easily understood time sheet. The time sheet is designed for submission on a monthly basis but the firm has arranged for the data to be submitted at fortnightly intervals. In spite of the fact that data is submitted fortnightly, staff should continue to complete time sheets each week.

Company notice quoted in *Weekend*

Under a State law in Colorado, housewives must obtain a small-game licence before they can buy mouse-traps.

Tit-Bits

A fire in Rio de Janeiro was caused, said the fire brigade, by 'total disregard for the most elementary rules of fire prevention.' The outbreak occurred at the Fire Prevention Institute.

Reveille

Since the former secretary had left the area and the former minutes could not be found, it was moved, seconded and carried that the minutes of the last meeting be adopted, as they would have been read had they been found.

Minutes of engineers' association

POLICE MOVE IN BOOK CASE

Headline in *Sunday Express*

85 per cent of the borough's 100,000 population is now treated at the new modern purification works at Waterloo.

Poole and Dorset Herald

He favoured long white flannels, striped jersey, and a blue-and-white cricket cap – beneath the bushiest red beard in the business.

Weekend

Shouts of 'Whites and Hongkongs go home,' echoed through the streets of Port Moresby in Papua, New Guinea, yesterday as crows, spurred by burgeoning nationalism, called for a black revolution and demanded the resignation of Chief Minister Michael Somare's coalition government.

Sunday Times

GARDENING AND LIVESTOCK. Will all clients of Miss S— please note that she is leaving town. No further stripping.

Newcastle Journal

Sidmouth warden, Mr Henry Y— needed help to maintain order and indecency in public places.

Pulman's Weekly News

An interesting case occurred several years ago in the *Eagle* boys' paper. The coloured centre-spread was a cross-sectional view of the latest technical wonder and I was always impressed by this work. The man responsible contacted the Ministry of Defence (Navy) to obtain drawings of nuclear submarines and was informed that only superficial sketches existed.

The artist obtained the slender information available and decided to design his own interior so as not to disappoint his boy readers. Positioning the nuclear reactors in what he thought was the obvious position he worked his way through the entire submarine.

On publication the balloon went up in the Ministry of Defence concerning what was thought to be a leak. The artist cheerfully explaining that he had designed his own nuclear submarine down to the crew's quarters was a performance well worth seeing.

Engineer

Woman guilty of trying to
kill her dead husband

Oldenburg, West Germany, Jan. 21. A 37-year-old woman has been found guilty of trying to kill her husband, even though he was already dead when she shot him.

Frau Ingrid Nicken was jailed for two years on a charge of attempted murder. She appealed against the verdict. According to evidence at the trial, she shot her husband twice in a rage after finding him sitting motionless in the kitchen one night after a drinking bout.

He had apparently died of a heart attack.

News agency

Africa arms dog Premier

Guardian

A Paris police superintendent was yesterday trying to decide whether a portion of cream cheese constitutes a dangerous police car.

Daily Telegraph

Luke Kelly as a woebegone tramp, has a bedpan, throwaway manner that is often funny.

Evening Standard

THIS IS THE HOUSE OF GOD
THIS IS THE GATE OF HEAVEN

This door is locked in winter
months

Sign on Cheshire church door

Boat for sale, one owner, green in colour.

Card in shop window

Dennis Harris, playing solo trumpet in the Bedford Band was awarded the medal for the best trombone player in the section.

Leigh Journal

Below is a 950-word palindrome compiled by Mr Desmond Grant of London SW15. The centre letter is set in bold type:

Smart regal rajahs, as a stalwart stressed at Radnor, in Wales, order a dismal celt to belt signora's animals, not a benign exile hero, nor pagan ayahs.

Evil, one pariah rapscallion at a fracas may rip at all, or rob at a party; raid a yard, stab, revile, or snipe nine italians.

Bad, sleek Cossacks amass at last, lob a bomb, attack a yak, mar pagodas, loot tenners, revel, debate rebate, jeer, upset a gang.

Isadora drank nips at a bar, stuns Mary. Ella snoops; Amos too; Stella sung a dirge. On a canal, pallid niggards yell.

Upstart enfeebled Omaha fools gab, gulp, snub, rebut, as liars leer sneer, gnaw, sniff. Upset, a deuce cad at Lima was.

A snug smug waster frets.

In a cabin, as Enid, rash, saw red, damn it Anita seems set on murders – but – examined, you bet all agreed stoor Keele, Belgrade, Cebu, Tarifa, snob nobs; big Slade men in Salta, Ragusa, Bute, Kansas, Prah; so many dim (alas, gone gaga) Rio, Crewe, Elba, Cannes, Topeka, Crete mates, Sir, assume Pamela-Anne is not to collect, nor fit to pillage kip, rone, vane, tags, tips, a plate, vodka, etna, velures, rohan, warp, a cang, ocelots, aster, fez; nor beer, trona, ether, a cape, savonettes, sack, rabot, tomboc, rotella, wax, oxo, fragaria, tug-tackle, a rare medoc, cab, otter, a batten, gardenia, cock, lisle, epee, potato, bass, some nitre, wolf, red lead, napery, tenon, a few eyas, tom-tom, a pome, parget, a bar, cage, pedal, bay, vines, ten egrets, yo-yo, soda; no bracelets, no mongrel, brawn, ray, nor tank, sump, mall, ramrod, ribes, rupee, taro, anna, cone, carbon, sard, a mare; nor knot, nor felt, tack, citrons, lioness, a burnet, talma, cleeks, wahoo, tupelo, pyrola, auk, stob, latakia, hog, a key, delf, fawn, a groat, corks, uta, a para, coot, tups, duster, rutela, panada, a turf, fur, anil, oak, rattan, a pane, ham, a desk, cots, rep, a taw, a camera, rasp, mats, spools, ten rugs, ten games, a cask, cups, pets, lyre, beet, test-tube, borax, oboe, mace, buck, cos, a gem, tuna, any metals, a pink, cola, pollock, card, a last, lamé, kale, perch, sal, a hare, game, opal, wallaby, olla, spacer, bassets, a plaid, drab, a tayo, two togas, passports, sage, cider, cans taps, snips, gum, nettle, pipe, keg, dulse, pastel, macle, macaroni, boron, Bible, balm, rocaille, macon, lias, gull, arums, dope, civet, argon, some mya, jam, upas, pansy, lilac, lath, crib, roselite, no hats, opah, sura, rial, geode; no roset, or sten, no belt, tiller, rosette, press, no melons, no gat, cote, llama, balsam, lemur, dossal, no bees, Roman ode, risotto, lace, raggee; not a trowel, capa, stone, dops, wad, a tract, rope, cigars, gold, rock, lime, tape, tar, tinsel, baths, a topsail, haddock, cod, dahlias, potash, tables, nitrate, pate, milk, cord, logs, rag, ice, port, cart, a daw, spode; not sap, a clew, or tat, one egg, areca, lotot, siredon, a morse, ebon, lasso, drum, elm, a slab, a mallet, octagons, no lemons, serpette, sorrel, little bonnets, rotes, or one doe, glair, a rush, a post, a hone, tiles, or birch, talc, a lily, snaps, a puma, jay, memos, no grate, vice, pods, mural, lugsail, no camellia, corm, label, bib, nor obi, nor a camel, camlets, ape, sludge, kepi, pelt, ten mugs, pins, spats, nacre, dice, gas, strops, sapsago, tow, toy, a tabard, dial, pastes, sabre, caps, alloy, ball, awl, a poem, a gerah, a lash, crepe, lake, malt, salad, rack, collop, a lock, nipa, slate, myna, a nutmeg, a sock, cube, cameo, box, a robe, butt, settee, beryl, steps, pucks, a case, magnets, gurnets, loops, stamps, a rare macaw, a taper, stocks, edam, a hen, a pan, attar, kaolin, a ruff, ruta, a dan, a pale, turret, suds, puttoo, carapa, a tusk, rocta, organ, waffle, dye, kago, haik, a talbot, skua, a lory, pole, putoo, haws, keel, cam, latten, rubasse, noils; nor tick, cattle, fronton, kroner, a madras, no brace, no canna, or a tee, purse, bird or marl, lamp, musk, natron, yarn, warbler, gnomon, stele, carbonado, soy, oyster, genet, sen, ivy, a blade, peg, a crab, a teg, rape, mop, a mot-

mot, say, ewe, fan, one tyre, panda, elder-flower, tine, moss, sabot, a topee, peel, silk, cocaine, dragnet, tabaret, tobacco, demerara, elk, catgut, air, a gar, fox, ox, a wallet, or cob, motto, bark, cassette; no vase, paca, reh, tea; nor tree, bronze, frets, a stole, cognac, a prawn, a horse, rule, van, teak, dove, talpa, spits, gate, nave; nor pike, gallipot, ti, front, cello, cotton, sienna, ale, map, emus, saris, seta, meter, cake, pot, senna, cable, ewer, coir, a gage, nog, salami, dynamos, harps, a snake, tuba, sugar, atlas, nine medals, gibs, bonbons, a fir, a tube, cedar, glebe, leek, roots, deer, gallate, buoy, denim, axe, tubs, red rum, notes, smee, satin, a tin, madder, wash, sardines, a nib, a canister, fretsaw, gums, guns, a saw, a milt, a dace, cue, dates, puffin, swan, greens, reels, rails, a tuber, buns, plug, bags, loofah, a model, beef, net, rats, pulleys, drag, gin, dill, a plan, a canoe, grid, a gnu, sallet, soot, soma, spoons, alley, rams, nuts, rabat, asp, ink, nard, a rod, a sign, agates, puree, jet, a beret, a bed, levers, rennet, tools, a dog, a pram, kayak, cat, tab, mob, a bolt, salt, ass, a mask, cassock, eels, dabs, nail, a tie, ninepins, roe, liver, bats, dray, a diary, trap, a tabor, roll, a tapir, yams, a car, fat, an oil, lac, spar, hair, a pen, olives, hay, a nag, apron, ore, helix, engine, batons, lamina, sarong, istle, bottle, clam, sida, red rose, lawn, iron, dart, a dessert, straw, lats, a sash, a jar, lager, trams.

Mid-Cheshire Central College
of Further Education

A MALE CLEANER BSc(Eng), C Eng, FIMechE, MIProdE is required for the Main College at Hartford.

Advert in *Northwich Chronicle*

Please carry dog or
hang on the hook on
the wall.

Notice in Bristol shop

Can you tell me why my sewing machine starts suddenly sewing with a mass of loops on the underside?

There could be many reasons. Whatever it is it requires adjusting by a sewing machine. We are sending you the names of two who are members of the Sewing Machine Dealers' Association.

Household hints column

Dear Sir, With reference to our letter re Majorca tour, the flight you mention is completely booked, but we will inform you immediately someone falls out, as usually happens.

Letter from travel agent

1969 Hillman Hunter. Auto saloon. One owner. God. Nominal mileage.

Biggleswade Chronicle

Win these Fabulous Prizes. Today's selection is 3 bottles of wine Pair of Giblets.

Cheshire paper

What does appeal to me is half an hour of passive exercise flat on my back, experiencing a sensation rather like a deep message.

Miss London

SILVERDALE, near Arnside.
Three-bedroomed cottage,
dully modernized.

Advert in *Guardian*

There was jubilation among the Fylde Conservatives, and deep disappointment for the Solicitors and Liberals.

Blackpool and Fylde Journal

Wanted by Georgie girl –
a right-handed carthorse

Daily Mirror

A post-mortem examination was held late yesterday by the senior Government pathologist, Dr J McNamara. But late last night the post-mortem had died.

The Age, Sydney

Two men were arrested on Thursday for the theft of a cart-load of girdles. If convicted, the FBI says, they face a ten-year stretch.

Philadelphia Inquirer

Figure Class I. A studio course working straight from the human figure. Anyone wishing to take advantage of the model without instruction may do so.

Art School brochure

In order to maintain a high standard of service to our customers, this branch will be closed all day on Thursdays.

Sign in Walton-on-Thames shop

Williams said he spent all the money on loving expenses and only £9 had been recovered, Sgt M— went on.

Evening Gazette

From the point of view of easy disposal the thief made a bad mistake, for paintings of our well-known Chairman and his wife would be very awkward things to dispose of locally.

Liverpool company's house journal

The defence claim that the words mhm mh mh mh h hm were no libel and that the words in their natural and ordinary signification were true in substance and in fact.

Irish Independent

Staffordshire Education Committee. Required for February: MISTRESS FOR PIANIST.

Wolverhampton Express and Star

COLLEGE REVOLT AS MAN IN WARDROBE GETS GIRL SUSPENDED

Headline in *Daily Express*

The British firm Digitronics Ltd has changed its name to Digitronix Ltd. To avoid confusion, it explains, with a US firm with a similar-sounding name.

Daily Mirror

If you suffer from seasickness, remember that deep breathing is a preventative. Take 15 to 17 deep breaths a minute instead of the usual 20, taking care to inspire as the vessel sinks and expire as she rises.

Long Island paper

Three fine goals from Frank Watts was indeed a tonic in this rain-lashed match, and his rat-trick had manager Jimmy Garson beaming at the finish.

Sunday Express

Archdeacon Turns Sod

Headline in *Barbados Advocate*

FOR SALE. Kenwood mixer, large size with all attachments including tooth extractor.

Glasgow Evening Citizen

The rule was that a girl would not be allowed in the bra without a man.

Exeter Express and Echo

Before starting to pray, either on the ground or from the air, operators should take account of wind conditions and their effect on drift.

Arcadian

Then, in not more than 15 words, say why you like to sleep between crisp, starched sheeps.

Torbay Post

Members of the County Council yesterday saw an exhibition to recognize the 500th title in the Ulverscroft Large Print book series. Mr F. A. Thorpe, publisher of the books, started with foul titles in September 1964. Now the large print books are known throughout the world.

Leicester Mercury

Signing the register after their wedding at the Sacred Heart Church, Paignton, are former Paignton beauty Richard William P— and Miss Maria Elizabeth S—.

Paignton News

A 31-year-old Baptist minister, married with four children, he made his first tour here carrying a wooden cross the length of Britain and Ireland.

Solihull News

When he arrived in Halifax the proportion of illegitimate births was 5.9 per cent. Now the figure was 13 per cent.

Halifax Courier

Revlon require a SENIOR BEAUTY ADVISER for a YORK STORE. Applicants should be mature cowmen.

Advert in *Yorkshire Post*

Investigations are pending of an application by the Potato Marketing Board and the National Farmers' Union for an anti-dumpling duty.

Yorkshire Post

First edition, profusely illustrated – *Unconventional Sex Practices*, spine cracked, appendix torn. $75.

American book catalogue

Chelsea College of Physical Education in Eastbourne is recovering with eight broken ribs in a clinic at Sierre in the Rhône Valley.

Evening Standard

TODAY'S SPECIAL

Steak O'Poivre

Menu quoted by 'Peterborough' in *Daily Telegraph*

Suddenly the taller of them, who had been doing all the talking, whipped round, produced a gun from inside his jacket, stuck it in my stomach, and hissed, 'OK, shut up or I will blow your brains out.'

Sunday Express

The Minister warned today that violent revolution in South Africa could only be avoided if racial injustice was stamped out there, with a 38 in. telescope.

Swindon Evening Advertiser

He was Chairman of Berwickshire Hunt Committee from December 1962. He rode regularly to hounds until his death would not allow him to do so.

Berwickshire News

Well-maintained 3-bedroomed house; 2 reception rooms, big kitchen; unusual offices.

South East London Mercury

If you bought our course: *How to fly solo in six easy lessons*, we apologize for any inconvenience caused by our failure to include the last chapter, titled: *How to land your plane safely*. Send us your name and address and we will send it to you post-haste.

Advert in *World Magazine*

The same was experienced by Mr and Mrs Pringle of the Kings Arms. They said their trade had improved recently renovated the old bar and lounge, and Mrs Pringle considerably.

Oxford Times

Johnson visited Sheffield with one intention – to do as much shoplifting as humanely possible, city magistrates were told yesterday.

Sheffield Star

HONEYMOON LUXURY FLAT
sleeps three

Advert in stationer's shop

'I sympathize with those people but this is not our responsibility because the land which is flooded belongs to British Rain.'

Southport Visitor

The children confide in the passenger on the train, who tells them he followed the trail and thinks their father is innocent. As this filf is directed by Lionel Jeffries it must have a happy ending.

Barking and Dagenham Advertiser

DANGER

WHEN RED FLAGS ARE FLYING
FLOODING OF THE RIVER
IS IMMINENT AND MEMBERS
OF THE PUBLIC MUST NOT
LEAVE THE RIVER BANKS

Sign near Leeds

FREE small flat wife to manage launderette.

Advert in *Evening Standard*

Accommodation includes large lounge, with two bay windows overlooking separate WC.

Advert in *The Stage*

The old stables are still in good condition and even the stalls and manager have been preserved.

Nottingham Evening Post

There is so much beauty in the world and there have been some beautiful films, really entertaining like *The King and I* and Doctor sex and violence all the time.

Folkestone, Hythe and District Herald

Late cinema – Tonight 11.15: Jack Lemmon and Shirley Maclaine in Billy Wilder's *Irma la Douche* (X).

Evening News

**Man is set free
in bullion case**

Guardian

Jones was jailed for a total of 18 months – six months for the burglary offence and two concurrent 12 months sentences for the fun offences.

Liverpool Echo

Bringing the four-hour meeting to a close, the remaining Labour members gathered their boots and papers together and left the chamber.

Keighley News

TEETH EXTRACTED
BY THE
LATEST METHODISTS

Sign in Hong Kong dentist's

She is an aspiring actress who dropped out of college and has only a soupcan of Indian blood.

Daily Mail

After a parade in which three medals were presented, Air Commodore Smith presented a local man, Corporal David Evans, with an award for 18 years long service and good conduct in the Officers' coffee room.

Grantham Journal

Cortina 1500 de luxe, 1968, taxed and tested, new engine 28,000 miles, excellent running order. oGod reason for selling.

Shields Gazette

The old Arley jerry was made redundant when a footbridge was built over the river Severn.

Wolverhampton Express and Star

After the escape the police set up a toad block.

Kent Messenger

These premises will shortly be opened as a cafeteria with courteous and efficient self-service.

Notice in Norfolk shop

'How dreadful is this place.' This melodious, thoroughly diatonic little piece is specially adapted for the dedication of a church.

Musical Times

We might quote you extracts from our roomful of testimonials, but an ounce of fact is worth a ton of fiction.

From a circular

London firemen with rescue gear were called early today to Dorset Street, Marylebone, when a man fell into a basement yard. He was lifted to road level, injured, and taken to hospital.

Daily Mail

```
Smoking is allowed as long as it does not
interfere with the work, but when the DSO
or any senior officers approach the
station it would be as well if they were
removed for the time being.
```

Army instruction

While a schoolgirl in Paris, Mrs Kennedy, who died in 1883, had the strange experience of carrying secret dispatches, bringing to England the first news of the escape of Napoleon from Melba.

Bedfordshire Standard

The ship was finally beached and the skipper's wife was brought safely to the local hospital. It was discovered later that she had been badly damaged in the beam.

Norfolk paper

BATHS, HOT AND COLD

Under the personal supervision of the proprietor.

Hotel advert

McVeigh hesitated. His eyes flickered over Reilly's face, dropped to the floor, went back to the papers. He picked them up, arranged them neatly, laid them down carefully.

Magazine story

Built on the lines of an old farmhouse kitchen, French girls in picturesque costumes flit about with cups of coffee and liqueurs.

Motor Cycle

One of Colorado's oldest citizens and a resident of Walsenburg for almost a century died here yesterday. Mrs Quintina was 104 years old at the time of her death, her grandmother said.

Brockson Enterprise-Times, Massachusetts

NOVEL EXPERIMENT IN A DORSET VILLAGE

CLEAN LIVING

Daily Express

The post office department has announced that while there will be no regular mail delivery on Thanksgiving Day, a skeleton will maintain service for special delivery and perishable material.

Parkersburg (Virginia) *News*

Pianos, mangles, lawn-mowers or other musical instruments will be welcome.

Parish magazine

A correspondent sends us the programme of a recent organ recital on a Sunday evening at a Staffordshire church, at which the selections were all by Wagner, except two by Tannhäuser.

Staffordshire Sentinel

FALSE CHARGE OF THEFT OF HENS

Police on wild-goose chase

Kent paper

In America it is true that our general rules of evidence and principles of law are mainly followed, and there is very little chance of an innocent defendant being acquitted.

Globe

All the bridesmaids wore red noses.

Birmingham paper

Prince Andrew was one of a party from Heatherdown School, Ascot, attacked by East End schoolboys who demanded their pocket-money. The incident happened in the National History Museum, but has been kept a close secret until now.

The Prince was not personally part of the museum.

Evening Standard

Due to an error Mr and Mrs E. Ankrum, 104 West Healey St, are the parents of a girl, born Tuesday morning in the Mercy Hospital.

Illinois paper

Mrs David Miller has a new baby boy at her house. Dave is just as happy as if it was his.

Ohio paper

Mary's eyes rested lovingly on the little gold brooch. 'Oh, Jack,' she murmured, 'it's the loveliest gilt I've ever had.'

Serial story

Birkenhead fire brigade were on the scene within a few minutes but by that time the fire had a good hold. Firemen were leaping up through the glass roof to a height of about fifty feet and streams of molten wax poured from the building.

Liverpool Evening Express

Perhaps you will be surprised to hear that for country week-ends she only wears lipstick. It's good to be young.

Woman and Beauty

On Monday Councillor Thompson's son will be married to the eldest daughter of Councillor James. The members of the Corporation are invited to the suspicious event.

Suffolk paper

The bride was dressed in a light place in the Wesley Temple in Minneapolis, with Dr James Brankburg, pastor, officiating.

Iowa paper

A specially qualified public health inspector has been sent to Orleansville to detect the presence of rats and eventually to work out a programme of extermination.

395 applications for adoption have been sent in to the authorities concerned and numerous offers of hospitality are being considered by the public health service.

Algerian paper

Speaking at Mablethorpe Council meeting, Councillor B— said: 'This Council is fiddling while Mablethorpe is settling under the pounding hooves of motorists.'

Local paper

New oblong woman's 9-ct
gold wristlet watch.

Advert in Yorks paper

Bearers carried his litter in teams of four, chanting: 'Oh Lord Buddha, lighten our load!' Mr Thomas said he lost fifteen pounds during the experience.

New York Herald Tribune

This work will afford protection from the smell which, when the wind is in the east, has caused ships to break away from their moorings often parting large hawsers.

Commercial weekly

'I used to think our prices were too high,' she said, 'but I'll never grumble again.' nmrdletaioicmrdysdshrdldcmrdl-paein.

Rochester (N.Y.) *Democrat & Chronicle*

Loudspeaker cars ordered spectators to keep at a safe distance until after the main blaze had been extinguished in five minutes, they were found hot and sizzling by ropes and dumped in Poole Park Lake.

Bournemouth Daily Echo

The bride carried a handsome bouquet of harem lilies.

North London paper

A Harrow Weald man raised a gate-post out of the ground and found a he said had a wife and a six-months-gold sovereign beneath it.

Evening News

At such times of self-renunciation in our own life, it is only supreme renunciation that appeals to us; and anything short of that, we feel, would be an inadequate support and stay for the soul. George Eliot realized this fact and showed it clearly in her portrayal of Maggie Tulliver in *The Milk on the Floor*.

New Reformer, Madras

ENID and JACK MYERS thank the Almighty for their recovery. They wish to express their deepest gratitude to their many friends for great help during this trying time. 'Good friends are priceless germs.'

Jewish Telegraph

ANTIQUE Drawing Room chairs £50. Shaise Lonuge (sofa) £65.

Herne Bay Press

The van was left unattended by the driver who went into a restaurant for dinner and later was found empty at Holloway.

Provincial paper

Will you also send me another cwt of your No 1 Ideal Meal. My wife asks me to say that she likes the food very much.

Advert in poultry paper

At 6.45 p.m. at the Young People's meeting, there will be a review of the first eight chapters of the Book of the Acts. The review will be in the form of a baseball game.

Battle Creek (Michigan) *Enquirer*

The Wilson County Baptist Fifth Sunday meeting will be held at Cedar Grove Baptist Church on March 3rd.

Visitors from other churches will be spread on the ground if weather permits.

Tennessee paper

Q. *What does the thread count printed on the label of sheets and pillowcases indicate?*

A. The massacre of Fort Mickinac in 1763 by Chief Pontiac of the Ottawas.

Columbus Citizen, Ohio

The vendor's solicitor will then send you the daft agreement and ask you to sign it.

Weekly paper

The Tasmanian wolf is striped like a tiger, has a tail like a rat, is a relative of opossums, and is the youngest man ever to be president of the United States.

Bridgewater (Connecticut) *Telegram*

Revolting police take over Bolivia

Iowa paper

Unaffectedly, Eva tossed aside many offers of movie, stage, and radio contracts, a magnet that was to gnaw later at her heart.

Journal-American

When Miss Dixie Janice Byram, daughter of Mr and Mrs R. C. Byram of this city, became the bride of Edward Hersey on Friday afternoon at 2 o'clock at many friends here occurred last overshirt of lace. Her hat was the First Presbyterian Church.

Winter Haven (Florida) *Herald*

Fire of unknown origin completely destroyed the home and contents of Mr and Mrs Stacey.

Corona, California paper

Widow seeks four mornings housework or would divide in two.

Advert in Sussex paper

'We didn't know he had what the poets call a Chilean heel – you know, a weak spot in the armour.'

Chicago Sun

The Fire Department was called to the home of Charles Hooper on Sunday for a chimney fire but did no particular damage.

Kennebuk (Maine) *Star*

When approaching roadways are wider than bridges, the accident rate is only about one-eighth, or less, than when the bridge is narrower than the approach.

Los Angeles paper

Another advantage of the new escalator is that any or all of the three staircases can be made to go in either direction at the same time.

Local paper

Many of our residents viewed the eclipse of the moon Monday night. The sun passed between the earth and the moon.

Greenup (Illinois) *Press*

This is the story of an advertising genius who works his way up from the position of errand boy to that of a greatly advertised food.

Calgary Albertan

Drop hot cooked rice into hot soap by spoonfuls and you will have rice dumplings.

Indiana paper

Council 'Digging Own Grave'

SMALLER BODY URGED

Ottawa Citizen

At Caxton Hall the conference was resumed of Municipal authorities interested in the conversation of old fruit, sardine, and salmon tins.

Birmingham Daily Mail

The famous composer, Karl Maria von Weber, was born in Eutin, Oldenburg, in 1786, a few weeks after the production in Germany, at Covent Garden, of his opera *Oberon*.

Indiana paper

The rain was responsible for certain other conditions that made the evening somewhat disappointing to the handful present. Two numbers, however, MacDowell's *March Wind* and Golliwog's *Cake of Debussy*, were particularly enjoyable.

North Carolina University magazine

The number of unvaccinated children born in Lambeth during the last three years averaged 800 a year.

South London paper

The marriage took place at Salter's Road Methodist Church, Gosforth, today, of Miss Gwendoline Dodds, Gosforth, and Lieut Frederick Dodds, of 6 Kensington Avenue, daughter of Mr and Mrs E. Robinson, son of Mrs E. Robinson, of 54 Bakewell Lane, Robinson. The bride was Darlington, and the later Mr attended by Mrs E. K. Rawlins and the best man was Lieut F. McCormack.

Northern paper

Discovered at 5.06 a.m. the flames starting on the third floor of the Midwest Salvage Co spread so rapidly that the first firemen on the scene were driven back to safety and leaped across three streets to ignite other buildings.

Cincinnati Times Star

Housekeeper wants post to businessman or respectable man.

Yorkshire paper

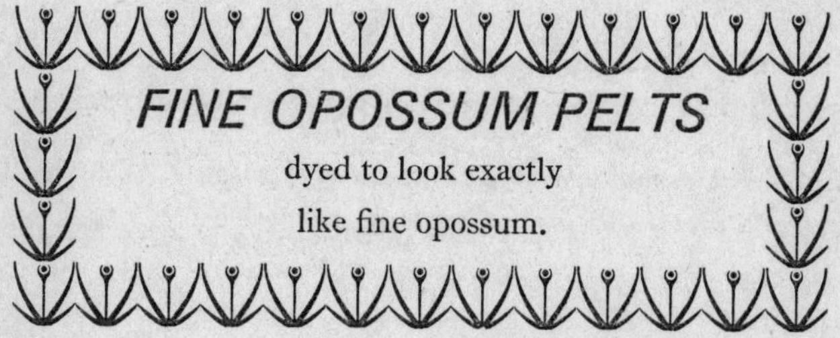

Advert in *Philadelphia Bulletin*

In the following pages I present half a dozen of my favourite 'Funny peculiars' from each of the four earlier books available in this series:

FUNNY HA HA and FUNNY PECULIAR

FUNNY HO HO and FUNNY FANTASTIC

FUNNY AMUSING and FUNNY AMAZING

FUNNY CONVULSING and FUNNY CONFUSING

Old readers may like to be reminded of them and the items will also serve as a trailer for new readers.

Sir, Traffic over the Channel bridge from England to France should proceed on the right, so as to prepare the drivers for the conditions they will meet when they arrive in France. Conversely, traffic from France to England should proceed on the left.

Yours truly, Derek E. Cox
The Times

Sir, Mr Green's interesting article: 'The trouble with cockroaches,' prompts the following story of an experience of a friend of mine some years ago. Returning late from the club one Saturday night he found everybody in bed, but his kitchen floor alive with cockroaches. Being of a tidy mind he sucked up as many as he could in a vacuum cleaner. Then the thought that they were not dead but merely snug in the cleaner prompted him to connect it by rubber tubing to a gas tap, and to fill the cleaner with gas. He retired happily to bed and slept late.

Next morning his wife found the cleaner and thought she would clean up a little; she switched on and it promptly blew up! The representative of the manufacturers was called in, and he confessed that he had 'never seen one go like that before'. My friend kept his silence and eventually got his replacement vacuum cleaner. I dare say any surviving cockroaches were highly amused. – R. J. MORLEY, 73 Egmont Rd, Sutton, Surrey.

Letter in *New Scientist*

Mrs George N—, a neighbour of Lord P— and 'Squire' of B—, has been running round her garden in the middle of the night . . . naked.

'I had an owl tucked under my arm,' she said by way of explanation.

Daily Mail

Sir, Miss H. B. Pang's fervent affirmations in defence of monocles for women (September 16) reminds me of a dear lady friend of mine, who did her shopping carrying an eight-day timepiece with an engine whistle firmly attached to it.

When a reporter from a local newspaper asked her why she carried these accessories, she replied that they were very useful. At any time, she explained, someone might stop her in the street and ask her if she possessed an eight-day timepiece with a whistle attached – and she could always say 'Yes'.

B. PAXTON, Clayton, Manchester
Letter in *Picture Post*

The plaintiff, giving evidence, said that when he was on the crossing in Chertsey Street, Guildford, he heard a shout. He turned and saw the cow coming pell-mell round a corner. It trampled over him and continued on its way. He did not think it deliberately went for him.

MR PATRICK O'CONNOR, for King Bros, submitted that the person in control of a tame animal *mansuetae naturae* – and a cow was undoubtedly tame – was not liable for damage done by it which was 'foreign to its species'. He would seek to prove the cow attacked the plaintiff; if that were so, there was no liability.

HIS LORDSHIP – Is one to abandon every vestige of common sense in approaching this matter?

COUNSEL – Yes, my Lord.

The hearing was adjourned.

The Times

'The boy would be expected to foresee,' Judge Forbes added, 'that there is one thing a man does not want after having his Sunday dinner; that is to have his feet tickled.'

News of the World

Sir, In last Sunday's issue you published a reproduction of Dame Laura Knight's boxing sketch of one of the successful entries in the Olympic Games Fine Arts Competition, to be seen in the Sport in Art Exhibition at the Victoria and Albert Museum.

My Association controls and regulates amateur boxing at the Olympic Games and in the 41 countries who are affiliated to us; and I therefore feel it my duty to point out that the boxers in the sketch are committing the following offences: (1) Holding; (2) Improper use of the hand (both boxers); (3) Extending a stiff arm under the opponent's arm; (4) 'Wrestling'. It is possible that the boxers are also delivering the kidney punch and the rabbit punch, but one cannot be certain of this.

I do not presume to criticize the sketch as a work of art, but it is regrettable that an exhibition which is designed to portray amateur sport in its highest forms should have included an example which degrades the noble art of self-defence to the level of a free-for-all rough and tumble. Yours, etc, RUDYARD H. RUSSELL, Lt-Col, Honorary Secretary-Treasurer, Association Internationale de Boxe Amateur.

Letter in the *Observer*

Dear Sir,

I have the honour to resignate as my works are many and my salary are few. Besides which my supervising teacher makes many lovings to me to which I only reply, 'Oh, not, Oh, not.'

Letter from Filipino woman teacher

Said Mr Justice Vaisey: 'It is a fearful thing to contemplate that, when you are driving along the road, a heavy horse may at any moment drop from the sky on top of you.'

Daily Graphic

Old-established manufacturer of suspension bridges requires door-to-door salesman.

African paper

CURRY EATING SPECIALIST IS FINED £5

A stranger in an Indian restaurant in Southend tried to demonstrate to Mr Arthur Flint how he should eat his curried chicken and rice. Mr Flint demonstrated his displeasure by pushing the curry in his face. In return, Mr Flint received a blow on the head with a chair.

At Southend court today the stranger, William Parkins, aged 28, a paint-colour matcher, of Boston Avenue, Southend, pleaded guilty to assaulting Mr Flint and was fined £5 with £3 3s. costs. Mr R. A. Shorter, prosecuting, said Mr Flint and a friend had ordered a meal when Parkins, sitting at a nearby table, spoke to them. He sat down uninvited and advised Mr Flint to drink a glass of water before eating the curry. Then he said he would show him how to prepare the meal, picked up the rice and poured it on the curry, and mixed it together. Mr Flint sat watching and then asked, 'Have you finished?' Mr Parkins said he had, whereupon Mr Flint picked up the plate and pushed it into his face.

The curry and rice ran down Parkins's clothing and following an argument, he left. Later, as Mr Flint sat eating a replaced meal, he felt a severe blow on the head and shoulders and on grappling with his assailant, found he had caught hold of the curry-stained Parkins. Police were called and Parkins told them, 'I hit him with a chair. My pride couldn't take it. He pushed me too far.'

In a statement he explained that he was only showing Mr Flint how to prepare his meal and added, 'He picked up the plate and pushed the whole lot in my face. I was shocked beyond belief because he seemed so friendly.'

Evening Standard

Rusty, a pony owned by a 16-year-old grammar-school girl Elizabeth Millbank, of East Street, Blandford, Dorset, is terrified by fireworks. So on the 5th November she will sit with him and read Shakespeare aloud.

Daily Mail

WIFE AGREED TO BE HIT ON SATURDAYS

by our parliamentary staff

The new ground for divorce, that since the respondent has behaved so that the petitioner 'cannot reasonably be expected to live with the respondent', was retained in the Divorce Reform Bill yesterday by the Commons Standing Committee on the Bill, without a division.

Mr Abse (Pontypool, Lab) said that a woman called on him professionally, complaining about her husband. She was bruised and battered. He sent for the husband, whose solution was that he would be content to knock his wife about only on Saturday night, instead of every night.

When Mr Abse told the wife of this offer, she said 'Saturday nights only? That will do nicely.'

The Times (by permission)

Will the person who unknown to me returned the family album, horseshoe ring, 72-inch pearl beads, 2 side-combs set with brilliants, 36-inch pearl beads, PLEASE RETURN the 25th photograph of the condemned building corner Ivins and Oaks Avenues, opposite city line. Reward. Apply—.

Advert in *Philadelphia Record*

Madame Ivy Cannon, a charwoman employed at the Ministry of War, has been given two years' imprisonment plus a £500 fine for covering her jam-pots with top secret military documents.

Paris-Presse

Can one eat curtains?

No, in general one cannot; but it may be as well to say what happened to an experienced housewife. She wanted to wash her curtains. They were delicate, so she went about it with care, but there was no indication as to how they ought to be washed.

Was it the way she set about it, or the washing compound she used whose composition she did not know? Anyhow, her curtains turned into a kind of soft paste, something like cream cheese, which she put in a bowl to show to her husband. Then she went out to do her shopping.

As luck would have it, her husband returned before her, looked for her in the kitchen, and getting hungry while waiting, he cut a slice of bread to eat with this sort of cream cheese on the table.

'Even with plenty of salt and pepper, your cheese is quite insipid,' he said to his wife on her return . . . He retired to a night of anguish, and without even getting indigestion.

If textiles do not carry a label specifying precisely how they should be washed, should they be marked 'eatable' or 'uneatable?'

translated from *J'achète mieux*,
the Swiss equivalent of *Which?*

I read with interest of the lady golfer who, when confronted by a naked man wearing only a bowler hat, asked him whether he was a member, and then hit him with a Number 8 iron.

Purists will long dispute whether it was obviously a mashie-shot, or whether the niblick should have been used. I hold no strong views myself, but I do wonder what the lady would have done had the man produced from his bowler hat a valid membership card.

Letter in *Daily Mail*

HUSBAND MIAOWS UNDER THE BED

The cat noises that came from under a young wife's bed kept her awake for months. They also gave her a headache – for the plaintive mewing was being made not by a cat, but by her husband. Every night, instead of getting into bed, he curled up under it . . . and just miaowed.

In desperation the wife asked a lawyer if she had grounds for a separation. 'My husband is a good and kind man, but rather shy,' she said. 'When it gets dark he stops talking and starts miaowing.' The astonished lawyer decided that the only complaint she could give was, 'My husband thinks he is a cat and prefers to sleep under, not in, my bed.'

Now a court in Imperia, Italy, will be asked to decide whether a husband's miaows in the night constitute grounds for legal separation.

Daily Mirror

ALTHOUGH written many years ago, *Lady Chatterley's Lover* has just been re-issued by Grove Press, and this fictional account of the day-by-day life of an English gamekeeper is still of considerable interest to outdoor-minded readers, as it contains many passages on pheasant raising, the apprehending of poachers, ways to control vermin, and other chores and duties of the professional gamekeeper.

Unfortunately, one is obliged to wade through many pages of extraneous material in order to discover and savour these sidelights on the management of a Midland shooting estate, and in this reviewer's opinion the book cannot take the place of J. R. Miller's *Practical Gamekeeper*.

Review in the American magazine *Field and Stream*

If you drive your car on to a policeman's foot – and don't remove it when he asks you to, are you guilty of assault? Three High Court judges yesterday disagreed on the answer to the question.

The Times

COLD SEX FOR TEA

HOUSEWIFE Mrs Rose C— bought an ice cream gâteau for tea at a village shop. When she opened the box at home in Duxford, near Cambridge, SEX stared her in the face – in large white letters across the top of the gâteau.

Mrs C— asked the makers, T. Wall and Sons for an explanation. They apologized, gave her another gâteau and told her that the letters had been put there in a fit of pique by a worker who had been sacked.

Daily Mail

A MOTORIST, THE LAW, AND AN ASS

If you have a donkey beside you is it safe to drive? Magistrates at Totnes, South Devon, had to decide this yesterday when a man appeared charged with not having proper control over his small Citroen car.

Peter Cox, principal of Dartington College of Arts, Dartington, near Totnes, pleaded not guilty to the charge.

Constable Kenneth Arthur told the Court, 'As the vehicle drew near I saw the backside and tail of a donkey through the windscreen and very close to the driver. On causing the defendant to stop, I confirmed that the animal was a donkey.' PC Arthur said the rear seat of the car had been removed and Cox's wife was sitting in the back holding the halter of the donkey, which was in a standing position. The front passenger seat had been removed. The prosecution contended that Cox did not have proper control because his visibility was restricted.

Cox said the donkey was very tame. He produced a photograph showing that the driver could see between the top of the donkey and the roof of the car and to either side of the car. While he was being cross-examined the Bench stopped the proceedings and dismissed the case.

Guardian

There were murmurs of disapproval from a defence solicitor. Mr Peter Smith, prosecuting for Havering Council, rose to inform puzzled magistrates, 'I think my friend is disturbed because the witness has taken the oath on a steak and kidney pie.'

Hornchurch Echo

MAN TRAPPED BY BEDSPRINGS FOR 5 DAYS

Mr Leonard Alcock, 63, of Britannia Road, Sheffield, was held prisoner for five days without food and water when his 30-year-old bed collapsed, plunging him among the mass of tangled springs. Neighbours, who realized he had not left home since last Wednesday, called the police.

Mr Alcock was released by ambulance men and taken to the Royal Hospital, Sheffield, given a check-up and a good meal and allowed to return home. He said yesterday, 'I went to bed to listen to the Celtic match on the radio last Wednesday and fell asleep. When I woke up I was down among the springs.

'I kept struggling to get free but the springs were too strong for me. I don't know what I would have done if the police hadn't come because I was getting weaker.'

Daily Telegraph

If he's stopped breathing, remove any obstruction such as false teeth or food, and immediately apply the 'kiss-of-life' (mouth-to-mouth breathing), the technique of which I'll describe next month.

Family Circle

Denys Parsons

Funny Ha Ha and Funny Peculiar 35p

Here is a superb collection of clangers and items of rare fascination – all taken from newspapers and other published sources. One side of each two-page spread is devoted to Funny Ha Ha, the other to Funny Peculiar. The result guarantees hours of hilarious and fascinating reading.

Funny Ho Ho and Funny Fantastic 35p

For your further enjoyment here is another collection of howlers and misprints. Funny Ho Ho on the left-hand pages; together with more Oddities and Absurdities, Funny Fantastic, on the right.

Funny Amusing and Funny Amazing 35p

A side-splitting companion to the impartial, impenitent and, occasionally, improper collections of Denys Parsons. The left-hand pages in this fresh collection of laughable bloomers and blunders are Funny Amusing, the right-hand pages Funny Amazing. Combined, they bring unending merriment and delight.

Funny Convulsing and Funny Confusing 35p

A rollicking new collection of boners and bungles, gaffes and giggles. The right-hand pages are Funny Convulsing, the left-hand, Funny Confusing. So take your pick of Denys Parsons – Mr Laughter Unlimited . . .

James Herriot

If Only They Could Talk 60p

The genial misadventures of James Herriot, a young vet in the lovely Yorkshire Dales, are enough to make a cat laugh – let alone the animals, if only they could talk.

It Shouldn't Happen to a Vet 60p

'Imagine a *Dr Finlay's Casebook* scripted by Richard Gordon and Thurlow Craig and starring Ronnie Corbett and you will understand why James Herriot is on to a winner . . . a delightful new collection of stories' SUNDAY EXPRESS

Let Sleeping Vets Lie 60p

The hilarious revelations of James Herriot, the now famous vet in the Yorkshire Dales, continue his happy story of everyday trials and tribulations with unwilling animal patients and their richly diverse owners.

Vet in Harness 60p

With the fourth of this superb series, James Herriot again takes us on his varied and often hair-raising journeys to still more joyous adventures in the Yorkshire Dales.